155

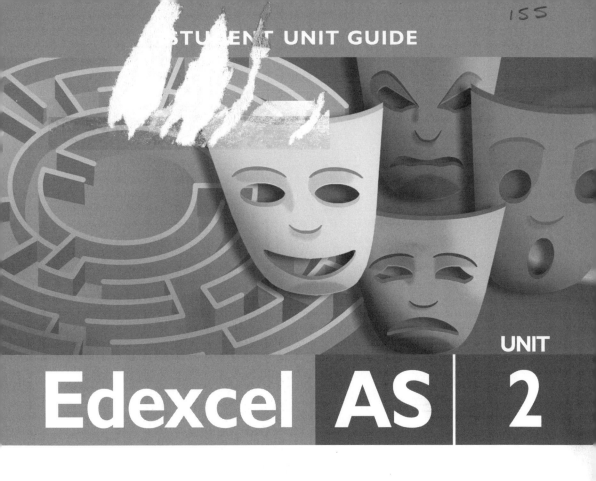

Edexcel AS | UNIT 2

Psychology

Understanding the Individual

Christine Bra

D1352018

Philip Allan Updates, an imprint of Hodder Education, an Hachette UK Company, Market Place, Deddington, Oxfordshire OX15 0SE

Orders

Bookpoint Ltd, 130 Milton Park, Abingdon, Oxfordshire OX14 4SB

tel: 01235 827720

fax: 01235 400454

e-mail: uk.orders@bookpoint.co.uk

Lines are open 9.00 a.m.–5.00 p.m., Monday to Saturday, with a 24-hour message answering service. You can also order through the Philip Allan Updates website: www.philipallan.co.uk

© Philip Allan Updates 2009

ISBN 978-0-340-94881-1

First printed 2009

Impression number 5 4 3 2

Year 2014 2013 2012 2011 2010 2009

This guide has been written specifically to support students preparing for the Edexcel AS Psychology Unit 2 examination. The content has been neither approved nor endorsed by Edexcel and remains the sole responsibility of the author.

Printed by MPG Books, Bodmin

Hachette UK's policy is to use papers that are natural, renewable and recyclable products and made from wood grown in sustainable forests. The logging and manufacturing processes are expected to conform to the environmental regulations of the country of origin.

Contents

Introduction

■ ■ ■

Content Guidance

■ ■ ■

Questions and Answers

Introduction

About this guide

The aim of this guide is to provide you with a clear understanding of the requirements of Unit 2 of the new Edexcel AS psychology specification and to advise you on how best to meet these requirements.

This guide looks at:
- the psychology you need to know
- what you need to be able to do and what skills you need
- how you could go about learning the necessary material
- what is being examined
- what you should expect in the examination
- how you could tackle the different styles of exam question
- the format of the exam, including what questions might look like
- how questions are marked, including examples of answers, with examiner's comments

How to use this guide

A good way to use this guide is to read it through in the order in which it is presented. Alternatively, you can consider each topic in the Content Guidance section, and then turn to the relevant question in the Question and Answer section. Try to grade your own answers. Working with someone else is more enjoyable than working alone and will mean you are actively learning — for example, try explaining the material to others, as this is an effective way of learning. Have your textbooks available too — you will need access to all the relevant information.

Study skills and revision strategies

If you have been studying the Unit 2 material, and have engaged in a reasonable amount of learning up to now, you can make good use of this guide. It can also help if you know little of the material and have only a short time before the examination.

Before reading on, answer the following questions:
- How long is left before the exam?
- Do you have a revision plan?
- Are you stressed and in a panic?
- Can you stick to your plan and trust it?

If you need to, draw up a revision plan now, remind yourself that you want to succeed, and practise some relaxation techniques.

introduction

How to learn the material

- Make your own notes and use these for your final revision.
- Have a separate sheet of paper for each approach.
- For each approach, note down the six headings (see the summary at the start of each approach) and use that as a guide. Leave room to fit your notes in under each heading.
- Read through each section, then make very brief notes as needed.
- Be sure to make notes on evaluation points.
- Finally, note down briefly three things about a key issue that describe the issue, and six 'facts' linking concepts to the issue.
- Another useful method is to use cards for each topic. Have the topic heading on one side of the card and brief notes on the other. Remember to note down equal amounts of knowledge and evaluation.

Revision plan

- Start at least 4 weeks before the exam date.
- Using times that suit you, draw up a blank timetable for each of the weeks.
- On the timetable, fill in all your urgent commitments (cancel as many plans as you can).
- Divide up what is left, allocating slots to all your subjects as appropriate. Don't forget to build in meal times, breaks and time for sleep.
- Stick to the plan if at all possible, but if you have to, amend it as you go.
- When studying, have frequent, short rests, and no distractions.

Time management

Answer the following questions to see how good you are at time management:

(1)   Are you usually punctual?
(2)   Do you tend to work fast and then correct mistakes?
(3)   Do you often put things off?
(4)   Do you feel stressed because you never have enough time?
(5)   Do you work slowly and carefully, and try to get things right first time?
(6)   Do you daydream?
(7)   Are you forgetful?
(8)   Do you find it hard to get started?
(9)   Do you keep your desk tidy?

Score 0 for 'yes' and 1 for 'no' to questions 1, 5 and 9. Score 1 for 'yes' and 0 for 'no' to questions 2, 3, 4, 6, 7 and 8. A score of 3 or below means quite good time management; a score of 4 and above means you need to work on it.

Relaxation techniques

If you would like to learn some relaxation techniques, look some up on the internet or refer to the Unit 1 study guide if you have it.

Examination structure and skills

Three approaches, six areas within each

Unit 2 consists of questions split into three different types ranging across the three approaches. Some material from Unit 1 is asked for as well, as you can see from the specification; this material is also covered in this study guide to help you to revise it.

The three different types of question are multiple-choice, short-answer and extended-answer questions.

Within each approach there are six areas:
- key terms and the basics of the approach (definitions)
- methodology
- content
- two studies in detail
- a key issue
- a practical

There might be questions for which you have to make links between the approaches; for example, you are asked to study three different explanations of gender. The three approaches for Unit 2 are the psychodynamic approach (Freud), the biological approach and the learning approach. You need to be prepared to answer a question on any of the six main areas for any of the three approaches. However, if you are asked a question about a key issue in the psychodynamic approach, you are unlikely to be asked a 'key issue' question for the learning or biological approaches.

Exam structure and assessment objectives (AOs)

Each of the two AS exam papers has multiple-choice questions at the start, followed by some short answer questions, some extended writing questions, and a 12-mark extended writing question (essay question) at the end. It is not possible to guess what will be on the paper — don't try. Prepare answers for all possible questions. The only guarantee is that there will be the three types of question (multiple-choice, short answer and extended writing), and a 12-mark essay question at the end of each paper.

Each paper will be different, and you have to be prepared to answer whatever questions appear. For example, there are many ways that short answer questions can be written, such as:
- 'Explain what is meant by...'
- 'Describe the procedure of...'
- 'Outline the theory...'
- 'Outline two weaknesses of...'
- 'What is the hypothesis in this study...?'

Read the question carefully and do what is asked, and you will do well.

Assessment objectives

The assessment objectives are listed in the specification. A brief explanation is given below, but check the full list of what you will be assessed on.

Assessment objective 1: knowledge and understanding (AO1)

- You need to recognise, recall and show understanding of psychological know-ledge, including theories, studies, methods and concepts, as well as psychological principles, perspectives and applications.
- You must communicate clearly and effectively, and present and select material well. For example, if you are asked to explain what is meant by social learning theory for 3 marks, and you just say that it is about social learning, you have not explained anything. You need to make your points clearly — for example:

> Social learning theory is about learning by observing others and then repeating the behaviour on some other occasion. Features of the theory include modelling and imita-tion as well as role models, whose behaviour is copied. There is also vicarious learning, which means that if observed behaviour is rewarded this behaviour is likely to be repeated in anticipation of the reward.

- You may miss out on marks by using bullet points, so avoid them. The problem with bullet points is that they encourage shorthand, meaning that your answer will not be clearly and effectively communicated.

Assessment objective 2: evaluation and comment (AO2)

You must be able to:

- analyse and evaluate psychological theories and concepts, referring to relevant evidence
- apply psychological knowledge and understanding to unfamiliar situations
- assess the validity, reliability and credibility of psychological knowledge

Assessment objective 3 (AO3)

You must be able to:

- describe ethical, safe and skilful practical techniques and processes, including selecting appropriate qualitative and quantitative methods
- know how to make, record and communicate reliable and valid measurement, using primary and secondary sources
- analyse, explain, interpret and evaluate methodology, results and impact of both your own practicals and the studies of others

The Unit 2 exam

Unit 2 is assessed in a 100-minute exam. Answers are written in a booklet similar to those used at GCSE. There are 80 marks available. This means you need to score around 1 mark per minute, with 20 minutes to spare for reading and thinking. In general, you can expect to gain 1 mark for each point that answers the question, or for elaboration of a point. Answers must be communicated 'clearly and effectively' (see AO1 above). Avoid one-word answers unless they are asked for. The final essay question is worth 12 marks.

Overall:
- one third of the marks (around 26 marks) are awarded for knowledge and under-standing (AO1)
- one third (around 26 marks) are for evaluation and comment and application to unfamiliar situations (AO2)
- one third (around 26 marks) are for knowing about and assessing practical work, both your own and other people's

With regard to the split over the type of questions, about 18% (around 14 marks) are for multiple-choice questions, about 50% (around 40 marks) involve short answer questions, and the remaining 32% (around 26 marks) involve extended writing, including the 12-mark essay question at the end.

In practice you should focus on revising equal amounts of AO1, AO2 and AO3 (know-ledge, evaluation and practical work) and just answer each question as it arises.

Two types of marking

There are two types of marking. One type is point-based marking, where 1 mark per point made is awarded, and there are also marks for elaboration and saying more about a point. The other type of marking is called 'levels'. In this type, bands of marks are awarded according to the quality of the answer.

An example of marking might be the mark scheme for a question asking for the independent variable (IV) for one of your studies, for 2 marks:
- 0 marks — no appropriate material (e.g. giving the dependent variable, DV)
- 1 mark — not fully operationalised, such as giving one side of the IV
- 2 marks — fully operationalised, giving both or all sides of the IV; possibly an example is given

Questions about your own practicals are marked according to levels and the quality — for example, if you are asked about planning a study using the biological approach, a thorough answer will get full marks and a weak answer will get few marks.

The essays are also marked using levels and according to quality. For example, if you are asked about two explanations for gender development and you only discuss one explanation you will be somewhere in the middle band.

It is in the levels marking that your written skills are assessed, including how well you select material for your answer, and what your spelling, grammar and use of terminology are like.

AO1, AO2 and AO3: getting it right

The key words in the question (called **injunctions**, e.g. 'outline') guide what you need to write. If you answer the question, you will do what is required and should cover the AO1, AO2 and/or AO3 skills.

Table 1 shows some examples of how AO1 injunctions are used and Table 2 shows examples of AO2 injunctions. Table 3 shows some examples of AO3 questions, which can include all sorts of injunctions but must be about practicals and methodology in some way.

Note that it is not so much the word itself (e.g. 'describe') that makes it AO1, AO2, or AO3, as the whole question.

The figures in brackets suggest the mark allocation you might expect for such a question.

Table 1 Examples of AO1 questions/injunctions

Type of question	What is being asked for
Describe (a theory)… (4)	Say what something is (a theory in this case). Imagine describing the theory to someone who knows little about the subject.
Identify a theory… (1)	Give enough information so that the examiner can understand what is being referred to. For example, if asked to identify a learning theory, an answer might be 'operant conditioning'.
Name a theory… (1)	Name a theory by giving the right term, such as 'classical conditioning' or 'social learning theory'. Use the name of a psychologist if there is one name associated with the theory, though this is not always the case. Freud's theory, for example, is suitable if asked within the psychodynamic approach.
Outline a definition of the…approach (2)	Follow the instructions for 'describe', but remember that this injunction requires less detail, and hence carries fewer marks.
Describe Freud's Little Hans (1909) study… (5)	Try to give the aim of the study, the case description, case analysis and the conclusion(s). (*Note that this is a case study so it is a bit different from the aims, procedure(s), result(s) and conclusion(s) of any other study.*)

Table 2 Examples of AO2 questions/injunctions

Type of question	What is being asked for
Outline a strength of… (2)	You are asked to outline something, so the injunction seems to be AO1 (i.e. knowledge and understanding). However, as what is outlined in this case is a *strength*, you are being asked to evaluate something, so this question would carry AO2 marks.
With regard to the stimulus material above, explain… (6)	You are asked to refer to some stimulus material and apply your knowledge of psychology to explain the material in some way. Refer to the material at least once in your answer.
Compare two theories of learning… (6)	You are asked to choose two theories of learning and then write about how they are similar and/or how they are different. 'And/or' means you can do both or one or the other.
Assess how far social learning theory is a useful theory… (4)	You are asked to consider practical uses of the theory of social learning or you can evaluate the theory itself, because that would shed light on how useful it might be — but focus on its usefulness.

Table 3 Examples of AO3 questions/injunctions

Type of question	What is being asked for
Outline the aim(s) of your experiment... (2)	You are asked to say what the purpose of your study was, which is to say briefly what you were trying to find out. 'Outline' sounds like an AO1 injunction, but as this is about your practical, it is an AO3 question.
Evaluate one of these studies — either Raine et al., Gottesman and Shields or... (5)	You have to have covered one of these studies but not all of them. Choose the one you know and give comments, criticisms, good points and so on about it. Consider strengths and weaknesses of the research method, perhaps, or criticisms of the ethics involved. Look at alternative findings or consider whether the conclusions drawn are justified. This is an AO3 question even though 'evaluate' sounds like an AO2 injunction. It is about someone else's study, which is psychology in practice, so it is an AO3 question. Raine et al. is explained in this guide.

Glossary

A list of terms used both for Unit 1 and Unit 2 is included at the end of the Content Guidance section. This is a list of definitions to help you in your revision. However, you can also use a glossary as part of your revision. Note Unit 1 terms are included here as well. If you are working with a friend, test each other by asking for the definition of 10 terms each, alternating and then reading out the term and checking the definition.

The glossary can be used to draw up revision cards. Write the term on one side and your own definition (formed by putting it into your own words) on the other side.

You could also go through the glossary matching terms to approaches, which will help your learning, picking out all the methodology terms to draw them together. Think of other ways of using the glossary. You could write out some definitions in your own words and, a few days later, identify the term being defined.

Content
Guidance

This section provides an overview of what you need to learn for Unit 2. You do of course need access to more material than is given here. Remember to prepare for AO1, AO2 and AO3 questions.

Structure of the AS units

Unit 2 comprises the psychodynamic, biological and learning approaches to psychology. Unit 1 is about two other approaches — the social approach and the cognitive approach.

Each approach follows the same format:
- definition and some specified key terms
- methodology (specified)
- content (some specified, some choice)
- two studies in detail (one specified and one other from a particular choice)
- one key issue (your choice)
- one practical (your choice — research method and some issues specified)

For each approach, suitable material is presented in this guide, but you may well have studied different examples where there are choices in the course. It might make sense to revise the material you chose for your course.

Methodology

The methodology covered in Unit 2 includes case studies, using inferential statistics and observations. Methodology covered in Unit 1 also needs to be revised for Unit 2, and some general principles about methodology are reviewed briefly here from Unit 1.

Key methodology evaluation terms

Methodology evaluation term	Explanation
Validity	Measuring what you claim to measure, meaning that what you measure is 'real life'.
Reliability	Getting the same results if you do a study again. To test for reliability there needs to be replicability.
Generalisability	The sampling is such that results can be said to be true of other people that the study is meant to represent.
Objectivity/subjectivity	An objective study is not biased because of the researcher giving their own opinions or influencing the results. Subjectivity is what occurs when the researcher affects the results by their own views.
Credibility	If the results are 'good' scientifically, they are credible. Also they are credible if subjectively we agree with them.

Exam preparation   List the above key methodology evaluation terms and define each for 2 marks.

Basic methodological features of a study

You will have learned a lot of the main features of studies. Revise those terms now to make sure you understand them clearly.

Key methodology description terms

Methodology description term	Explanation
Aim	A brief statement of what the study is intending to find, such as 'to see if females are better at verbal tasks than males'.
Alternative hypothesis	A carefully defined statement of what the study is aiming to find (the 'alternative' to the null hypothesis, which is defined later in this book). The independent variable (IV) and the dependent variable (DV) are both clearly stated. In an experiment the alternative hypothesis is the **experimental hypothesis**.
Operationalising	Making something measurable and clear. For example, to study the aim given above, brain lateralisation or use of language has to be measured.
Independent variable (IV)	The variable that the researcher manipulates (changes) to see the effect on the dependent variable. For example, when finding out whether males or females are better at language tasks the variable of interest is gender.

Methodology description term	Explanation
Conditions	An IV has more than one condition as it is about the different ways that X or Y would affect the DV. In the example used here one condition is females and the other condition is males.
Dependent variable (DV)	The variable that is measured to see the effect of the IV. In the example used here ability in language tasks is the DV. This can be made measurable by giving both males and females anagrams to solve, such as 'RNGEOA' and 'MLUSP' (which are fruit — orange and plums).
Control	The IV is changed and the DV measured, but everything else is controlled to make sure nothing else affects the results. For example, the experimenter makes sure that the same list of anagrams is used for each group (both males and females).
Situational variables	Variables in the situation such as noise, temperature and light might affect the results if they are different in the different conditions.
Participant variables	Variables in the participants such as mood, hunger, age or gender might affect the results if they are different in the different conditions.

Exam preparation List the above key terms and define each for 2 marks. Make sure you are able to give an example of each, as is done in the table.

Research methods

Each of the five approaches in your course focuses on a different research method (as well as different aspects of methodology).

The psychodynamic approach

Summary of the psychodynamic approach

Definition and key terms

The approach is defined in this section, and key terms are listed and briefly explained.

Methodology

The research method covered in this approach is the case study, both the case study in general and case studies as used by Freud. Other issues include evaluating the analysis of qualitative data, considering issues such as reliability, validity, subjectivity, objectivity and generalisability. The credibility of Freud's theory is considered, as well as ethical issues to do with case studies. Sampling techniques are revisited, though you will have covered them in Unit 1. Other methodological issues covered here include correlations and cross-sectional and longitudinal designs.

Content

Some of Freud's ideas are found within this approach, including his idea of five psychosexual stages, his personality theory referring to the id, ego and superego, his focus on what he called the Oedipus complex and his view of how gender develops within the phallic stage. Alongside that you are asked to understand defence mechanisms including repression and one other; the one chosen here is denial. For the biological and the learning approaches you will also look at ways of explaining gender development, among other things, and you will have to be able to compare these two explanations with Freud's explanation. How the three approaches explain gender is compared in the learning approach, because by then you will have revised all three explanations.

Two studies in detail

The main study is Little Hans (1909). You also need to study one other from Axline (1964), Bachrach et al. (1991) and Cramer (1997). Here Axline (1964) is chosen, but you may have studied one of the others.

Key issue

The issue chosen here is the debate concerning false memory and repression. You may have studied a different key issue for your course.

Practical

You will have carried out a practical within the psychodynamic approach that was a correlation, involving self-report data using two rating scales. You should use your own practical for the exam, because you will have 'learned by doing'. Some ideas about the practical are suggested in this book.

Definition and key terms

The psychodynamic approach focuses on the power of the unconscious, which governs about 90% of our thinking even though we are by definition unaware of it. For example, Freud thought the id was the demanding and wanting part of our personality, and all its wishes and desires are unconscious.

Another focus of the approach is on early childhood, because Freud held that the first 5 years are the most important in developing personality. The id (which develops first), ego (second) and superego (third) all develop in those first 5 years.

Exam preparation Define the psychodynamic approach and give two examples, for 6 marks.

Key terms

As with all five approaches, the psychodynamic approach has key terms that you need to be able to define and explain. These are the three parts of the personality (**id**, **ego**, **superego**), the five psychosexual stages (**oral**, **anal**, **phallic**, **latency** and **genital**), **defence mechanisms**, **repression**, **the Oedipus complex** and the three parts of the mind (**conscious**, **preconscious** and **unconscious**). The terms are explained as they appear.

Exam preparation Define each key term, including one example, for 3 marks each.

Methodology

Case studies

Freud's case studies are a little different from general case studies, so the two are explained separately here.

Case studies in general

- Case studies are in depth and are usually about one person or a small group.
- They gather a lot of data from many different sources and different research methods are used within the case study.
- When different research methods are used and the data compared, this is called triangulation.
- Case studies are known for gathering qualitative data to get the required depth and detail; there are often quantitative data as well.
- An example of a case study is that of Clive Wearing, a brain-damaged patient. He had a virus that damaged the hippocampus (in his brain), so that he was unable to form long-term memories from the information held in his short-term memory.

Strengths and weaknesses of case studies (other than Freud's)

Strengths	Weaknesses
• Data are valid because they are in depth, detailed and focus on real experiences in a real situation • A valuable research methodology because a case study may be the only way to gather rich, detailed qualitative information in context and with meaning for those concerned	• Lack generalisability because they are about one individual (or small group) only, so they are specific rather than general and data cannot be applied fairly to others • Hard to replicate, so cannot be tested for reliability, which means data may be subjective and cannot be used to build up a body of knowledge

Freud's case study method

- Freud's case studies gathered in-depth data about individuals.
- He gathered a lot of data using different research methods within the case study.
- The research methods he used included dream analysis with symbol analysis, free association and analysis of slips of the tongue — such methods coming under the heading 'psychoanalysis'.
- The people he studied were patients who came to him for analysis to solve unexplained physical problems or mental health problems such as phobias.
- An example of a case study that Freud carried out is Little Hans.

Strengths and weaknesses of Freud's style of case study

Strengths	Weaknesses
• Uses different methods to uncover unconscious wishes which are impossible to access by conventional means	• Involves subjective interpretation by the analyst, so it is not scientific

Strengths	Weaknesses
• Acts both as a research method and a therapy and allows the analysand to be cured	• Cannot be replicated to test for reliability because it focuses on the unique unconscious desires of an individual and the analysis is carried out by one therapist

Research methods used by Freud in his case studies

- **Dream analysis:** Freud listened to his patient's dreams, and he called what they told him the manifest content. However, uniquely, Freud then analysed the story of the dream to find the latent content. The latent content is material in the unconscious that is hidden in the dream. The manifest content includes symbols that can be interpreted, so this is a type of symbol analysis. The dreams of Little Hans were analysed by Freud.
- **Free association:** the patient is asked to 'tell' a stream of conscious thoughts. The analyst looks for links between the thoughts and between the words used for them, on the principle that linked words and thoughts show linked concepts, which can reveal unconscious thoughts.
- **Slips of the tongue:** Freud noted when someone said one thing while meaning another, such as using someone else's name or using the wrong word completely.

Exam preparation Describe the case study method: first in general, and second Freud's style of case study, each for 4 marks. Include an example in each case for 1 mark.

Exam preparation Evaluate the case study method: first in general, and second Freud's style of case study, each for 6 marks.

Analysis of qualitative data

You will have looked at how to analyse qualitative data when studying the social approach. For this section you need to know about how reliable, valid, subjective or objective qualitative data are as well as how generalisable they are when analysed.

Features of qualitative data

Feature	Applied to the analysis of qualitative data
Reliability	• Data are reliable if a study is repeated and the same results are found. In general, qualitative data are hard to obtain again because in another situation with another researcher someone might say something different. • For example, the Little Hans study could not have been replicated (repeated), as access to the parents would have been needed, and Little Hans was changing all the time. • However, Clive Wearing's memory difficulties can be studied more than once, so some case studies can be tested for reliability.
Validity	• Data are valid if they are about real situations and real people. In general qualitative data are about 'real life', because many different research methods are used to make sure data are not artificial. • However, Little Hans's dreams, comments, emotions and behaviour were reported to Freud through Little Hans's parents, so perhaps interpretation by the parents affected the validity of the data.

Feature	Applied to the analysis of qualitative data
Subjectivity or objectivity	• If a researcher affects the data by the way they gather or interpret them, the data are subjective. If there is no bias from a researcher or from other features of a study, the data are objective. Science needs objectivity. With qualitative data the researcher has to draw out themes, so there is possibly some subjectivity.
Generalisability	• Generalisability refers to how far the findings can be said to be true of other people. Qualitative data involve in-depth, detailed information about a unique individual or small group. They are therefore usually thought of as not generalisable because this uniqueness means the findings are also unique. • However, if there were similar cases and similar individuals, then perhaps the findings would be to that extent generalisable.

Exam preparation Explain each of the features in the table, writing enough to get 2 marks for each explanation. Also describe how qualitative data are analysed, for example using themes, for 4 marks.

Credibility

In the psychodynamic approach you have to study issues of credibility. There can be two elements to credibility. One element is how far someone subjectively believes some information and accepts it because it fits in with their beliefs and assumptions. The other element is more about objectivity and how far information comes from a good source with tested data.

Case study evidence tends to be seen as credible in the subjective sense because of the depth and detail about an individual (or small group). However, in an objective sense there is less credibility because interpretation is needed to analyse qualitative data, and questions might be asked about how far the study yielded unbiased data after analysis.

Freud's data have been said to lack credibility because he interpreted the data. He analysed dreams to 'find' symbols that hide unconscious thoughts, and there is no actual evidence about the unconscious.

Masson (1989) attacked Freud's views in three main ways, as shown in the table.

Masson's criticisms of Freud

Criticisms of Freud: lack of credibility	Explanation
Avoiding 'finding' child abuse	Freud interpreted any comments about parents involving sexual feelings or issues as being part of the Oedipus complex — they could have been about child abuse.
Abusing the power of the analyst	The analyst has power over the analysand and the analyst's interpretation may be accepted because of this power. This can lead to false memories, as seen in the key issue later.

Criticisms of Freud: lack of credibility	Explanation
Sexist	Freud focused on boys, through the Oedipus complex and castration fear. He thought the effect of the phallic stage (a male-oriented concept) on girls was much less important.

Exam preparation Make sure you know enough about the credibility of Freud's ideas, giving criticisms such as Masson's but also considering their strengths, to answer an essay question for 12 marks. The ideas' strengths and weaknesses can be used to discuss their credibility.

Ethics

The five main ethical guidelines were covered in the social approach, so review them now.

The five main ethical guidelines

Guideline	Explanation
Informed consent	Participants must agree to taking part and having their data used, knowing as much as possible about the study.
Deceit	There must be no deceit. Where deceit is necessary because otherwise the study would not work, there must be a full debrief.
Right to withdraw	Participants must be given the right to withdraw at any time, both during the study and afterwards, when they can withdraw their data.
Debrief	Participants must be fully informed after the study — of what it was about and where their findings fit. This is particularly important if there is deceit and, therefore, lack of informed consent.
Competence	The researcher must be competent to carry out the study. They must be sufficiently qualified and/or overseen by someone else. They must adhere to ethical guidelines and understand not only what they are doing, but also the consequences, which they must be equipped to deal with.

In the psychodynamic approach you are asked to look at two additional guidelines, linked to each other — privacy and confidentiality. Privacy means not making someone's identity known. It depends on confidentiality, which means not sharing data from individuals with anyone else without asking the 'owner' of the data first. If information is to be made public, the identity of the participant has to be protected.

The rules relating to privacy and confidentiality are:
- Keep appropriate records, safely and in accordance with data protection rules.
- Only reveal information that the participant or client has given permission for, or is within professional areas.
- Obtain consent directly where possible or from someone acting on behalf of the participant or client.
- Inform the participant or client from the start about what data will be gathered, where it will be kept, and what purpose it will be put to.

- Only breach confidentiality if someone's safety is involved — which could be the participant or client, or could be someone else.
- In such cases consult with a colleague.
- Make sure everyone working with the person is aware of privacy and confidentiality procedures.

Exam preparation Prepare a 12-mark essay on ethics and psychology in general, as this will help you to organise your thoughts. Include issues such as why there are ethical guidelines, and give examples of studies that are ethical (or not).

Cross-sectional and longitudinal designs

In studies with a cross-sectional design, data are gathered at one moment in time from different groups of people so that one group is compared with another group on the same task. An example is to compare 5-year-old children with 8-year-old children to see their level of language ability.

Strengths and weaknesses of cross-sectional studies

Strengths	Weaknesses
• They are reasonably cheap, quick and practical because there is no follow-up and participants are only tested once • Participants are found more easily because there is no follow-up; this makes the studies more ethical because there is less pressure on participants than there is in longitudinal designs	• There is not as much detail as in a longitudinal design with regard to individual differences • They are snapshots that gather data at one moment in time; they cannot easily gather data about trends in development

Longitudinal designs are the opposite of cross-sectional designs. These involve gathering data from the same people undergoing the same test or tests at different times. An example is to test a group of 5-year-old children for language ability and then test that same group again when they are 8 years old.

Strengths and weaknesses of longitudinal studies

Strengths	Weaknesses
• The same participants are followed, so there are no participant variables to be considered and conclusions can be stronger than in an independent groups design • They are probably the best way of studying developmental trends because they repeat the tests or tasks over time and comparisons can be drawn	• The participants may not want to continue or may move away; those remaining may share characteristics that mean the findings are biased • There are practical difficulties; they can be expensive, time consuming and the researchers may change

Sampling

You looked at the four types of sampling when you studied social psychology, and there is no new material here. Sampling is used when you want to test a large population: because there are too many people to test individually, you have to choose a small number to represent the target population.

- **Random sampling** means that everyone in the target population or sampling frame has an equal chance of being picked to be in the sample.
- **Stratified sampling** means generating categories that fit the aim(s) of the study, for example age, gender, occupation or whether someone drives or not.
- **Volunteer/self-selected sampling** means asking people to volunteer. If a questionnaire is sent out by post, those returning it will by definition have volunteered.
- **Opportunity sampling** means that the researcher takes whom they can find.

Strengths and weaknesses of sampling methods

	Strengths	Weaknesses
Random sampling	• Low bias because everyone has an equal chance of being chosen • Sample can be checked mathematically for bias	• Cannot be certain that the sample is representative of all groups/types etc. • Difficult to access all the population so that random sampling can take place
Stratified sampling	• All relevant groups/strata will have at least some representation • Limits the numbers of participants needed	• It is difficult to know how many of each group is needed in order to represent the target population accurately • Relies on researchers knowing all the required groups/strata; forces choice of participants and proportions of all groups so can give bias by excluding people
Volunteer/self-selected sampling	• Ethically good because people volunteer, so are willing to be involved • More likely to cooperate, which means there may be less social desirability and such biases	• Only certain types of people may volunteer, so there is bias • May take a long time to get enough volunteers
Opportunity sampling	• More ethical because the researcher can judge if the participant is likely to be upset by the study or is too busy to take part • The researcher has more control over who is chosen and should, therefore, be able to get the sample quickly and efficiently	• Only people available are used and they may be a self-selected group (e.g. not working, so available during the day) • May not get representatives from all groups so there may be bias

Correlations

The practical you will have carried out for the psychodynamic approach was a correlation. One way of gathering correlation data is to use self-report data and rating scales.

Self-report data are obtained when participants judge themselves on some category or categories — they report on themselves. Any scale where the participant has to rate something is a rating scale, for example judging someone's attractiveness on a scale of 1 to 5.

In studies with a correlational design, one participant gives two scores. For example, two scores could be age and the number of words that can be recalled from a list. So for each participant, both these scores are found. Perhaps the older someone is, the fewer items they can recall, and this would be a correlation. Another example of a participant's two scores could be one for their happiness rating and one for their length of time in a relationship. Perhaps the longer someone is in a relationship the happier they are.

Negative correlations are when one score rises as the other falls. An example would be: the higher the age, the lower the number of items recalled from a list.

Positive correlations are when as one score rises the other rises as well. An example would be: the higher the happiness rating, the longer the relationship.

Correlations are about maths and statistics and are presented in that way. A perfect positive correlation is +1 and a perfect negative correlation is –1, with 0 being no correlation at all. A perfect positive correlation would be when in every case as one score rises the other rises too; and a perfect negative correlation would be when in every case as one score rises the other falls. Note that a negative correlation *is* a correlation. It is 0 that means no correlation at all — when there is no relationship. If the result of testing for a correlation is near +1 or –1 (e.g. 0.78) it is a fairly strong correlation. The nearer it is to 0 (e.g. 0.20) the weaker the correlation.

Strengths and weaknesses of correlational design

Strengths	Weaknesses
• Good for finding relationships at the start of an investigation; also unexpected relationships; once two sets of data are collected from the same participants, a test can be carried out to see if there is a correlation between them • There are no participant variables, so yield more secure data	• Only suggests a relationship; this does not mean that the two variables are causally related; they may only show a relationship by chance or because of some other factor • Data may not be valid because the measures may be artificial or unconnected

Analysing correlations

To analyse correlations you need first to list both sets of scores and then rank each set of scores separately. After that, study the rankings — and look to see if high ranks go together and low ranks go together, or if high ranks go consistently with low ranks and vice versa.

Ranking data involves starting from the lowest score and giving that rank 1 and continuing. The only difficulty is if some scores are the same, in which case you give those scores the same rank, but in a way that keeps an equivalent number of ranks. So if there are three scores of 8 and they follow rank 3, you share out ranks 4, 5 and 6 between the three '8' scores, giving each a rank of 5. Then you carry on from rank 7. This is the same as finding the median of the scores because to find the median you have to rank the scores first.

How to rank scores

Scores	1	3	5	8	8	8	9	14	20
Rank	1	2	3	5	5	5	7	8	9

You can also draw a scattergraph of the scores and look at the line of best fit to see whether there is a correlation or not. The graph in Figure 1 uses a made-up set of scores, illustrating a positive correlation, and you can see how as one score rises the other rises too.

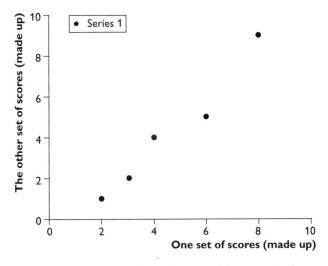

Figure 1 Scattergraph to show positive correlation

When you analyse a correlation, the scattergraph and a look at the rankings should tell you whether you are expecting there to be a relationship or not and whether it is likely to be a positive or a negative correlation.

You can also use statistical testing (e.g. the Spearman Rank Correlation Coefficient) to see if there is a correlation. How to use statistical tests is explained in the section on the learning approach.

Exam preparation Consider two question stems:
(a) Outline what is meant by… (3 marks)
(b) Show what is meant by…through the use of an example. (3 marks)
Apply them to the terms: longitudinal study, cross-sectional study, random sampling, systematic sampling, volunteer sampling, opportunity sampling, positive correlation, negative correlation, self-report data, ranking.

Content

You need to know about Freud's psychosexual stages, including the Oedipus complex and the three parts of the personality that fit into the stages. Your course also covers Freud's explanation of gender development, which is a key theme for Unit 2. And you need to know about two defence mechanisms, one of which is repression. Denial is the second defence mechanism chosen here, but you may have covered a different one.

The five psychosexual stages

The table below explains the five stages; the phallic stage is explored in more detail later in relation to gender development. Each stage (except the latency period, which is not really a stage) draws on sexual energy, which Freud thought was present at birth, and at each of the first three stages there is a different focus for this energy.

The five psychosexual stages

Stage	Description
Oral	The baby at birth is all id (see below) and demanding, working on the pleasure principle, and the source of pleasure at this stage is the mouth. This stage lasts up to about 18 months old.
Anal	The focus of pleasure in this stage is the anus and faeces. Potty training is an important feature, and if the training is too strict or too lenient this can cause problems. This stage lasts up to around 3 years. The ego (see below) is developing at this stage.
Phallic	This is an important stage according to Freud because the focus of pleasure is the genitals, and Freud thought that sexual instincts were important in forming the personality. The boy goes through the Oedipus complex (see below), involving castration fear. The girl goes through the Electra complex (though this did not come from Freud), involving penis envy. The superego (see below) develops at this stage. This stage is found between the ages of around 4 and 5 years old.
Latency	This is not really a stage as nothing happens with regard to shifting the focus of pleasure. Children make friends of the same sex. There is development of course, but not psychosexually. This stage starts after the Oedipus complex is resolved, at about 5 years old, and ends at puberty.
Genital	If the first three stages have been successfully passed through, particularly the phallic stage and the Oedipus complex, then at this stage the person forms relationships with the opposite sex and the focus of pleasure is again the genitals. This stage starts at puberty.

Becoming fixated at one of the stages

Fixation refers to not resolving issues in one of the stages and, therefore, being held back because of this. This 'holding back' means holding back energy to keep the personality balanced even though there is fixation, so resolving the issues later is important to maintain a healthy balance.

Adult character if fixated at one of the first three stages

Stage	Adult character
Oral	Obsessed with stimulation of the mouth, e.g. pen sucking and smoking. Oral fixation can lead to talking too much, over-eating, or being sarcastic (biting).
Anal	Anal-expulsive character is messy and might have 'messy' hobbies such as pottery/building. Anal-retentive character is stubborn and obsessively clean.
Phallic	Inappropriate learning of gender behaviour might lead to someone vain and self-assured, even reckless. The adult might not be capable of loving someone else.

The three parts of the personality

The table below explains the three parts of the personality; they can be linked to the first three psychosexual stages.

The three parts of the personality

Part of the personality	Description
Id	The demanding, 'I want' part of the personality, from birth, working on the pleasure principle.
Ego	The rational part of the personality, balancing either competing demands of the id or competing demands of the id and the superego.
Superego	Works on the morality principle and contains social rules and parent rules. The superego consists of the conscience (what is right and wrong, and that you should do right) and the ego ideal (what should be done and what the individual feels they should be like).

Defence mechanisms

Anna Freud, Freud's daughter, brought in the idea of defence mechanisms to help the ego to keep the peace between the demands of the id and the superego. Repression involves keeping thoughts in the unconscious and not allowing them into the conscious mind, as that protects the person from those thoughts, wishes and desires, and the ego does not have to deal with them. Denial is another defence mechanism: when something traumatic happens which would be hard to deal with, the person denies that it has happened at all. Again, this is not a conscious process; the person will not realise they are 'in denial'. Denial can protect a person from inappropriate sexual feelings, for example.

Exam preparation Describe both these defence mechanisms (or repression and one other) for about 4 marks. This can include an example, which is worth preparing in any case as you could be asked for one. Then say what defence mechanisms are (in general). You do not have to evaluate the idea of defence mechanisms.

Gender development according to Freud

In the phallic stage, according to Freud, children develop gender-specific behaviour alongside developing the superego. This happens when they identify with (become) the same-sex parent through either the Oedipus complex (boys) or the Electra complex (girls). Freud did not consider girls, in fact, and the Electra complex was developed later, but it is included here as part of the psychodynamic approach. You will need to be able to compare psychodynamic ideas about how gender develops with the explanations of the biological and learning approaches. This comparison is made in this guide in the context of the learning approach because you will have revised all the different explanations by then.

The Oedipus complex

Freud was hearing about sexual issues related to parents when children were around 4 or 5 years old. Freud explained this sexual focus by showing that the genitals were the area for sexual pleasure at the phallic stage at this age. Freud concluded that boys had sexual feelings for their mother, though unconsciously. This led to feelings of guilt and also fear of the father, whose place the boy wanted to take. The fear took the form of castration fear. Such fear and guilt was hard to reconcile so the boy resolved the conflict (the desires of the id conflicting with the conscience of the superego) by identifying with and 'becoming' his father. The boy, therefore, takes on the masculine behaviour of his father.

The Electra complex

Girls also focus on the genitals in the phallic stage and have feelings for their father. They understand they do not have a penis and develop penis envy, though this feeling is not as strong as castration fear so girls do not identify with their mothers to resolve their feelings as strongly as boys identify with their fathers. The girl focuses on her father because she thinks he will give her a penis. Some theorists have said that the replacement for a penis is a baby, so the girl unconsciously wants a baby and that is why she wants her father. Other theorists suggest that it is male power that a girl wants from her father. For one reason or another the girl wants the father, feels guilty about these unconscious feelings and resolves the demands of the id (the feelings) and the superego (the guilt) by identifying with the mother, taking on female norms, behaviour and beliefs.

Strengths and weaknesses of Freud's theory

Strengths	Weaknesses
• It allowed treatment for mental illnesses that were untreated at the time • The use of case studies allows valid data to be gathered and in-depth analysis to take place	• The findings are not generalisable because the data are about individuals and are specific to them • The methods are not scientific • The method requires interpretation and it is difficult to achieve objectivity, so the theory is not scientifically based • The sample is biased; this bias means lack of generalisability • The theory is limited because the study stops at adolescence, and focuses only on psychosexual development

Exam preparation There are many questions that can be asked about the three parts of the personality, the five psychosexual stages and how gender behaviour develops in the phallic stage. You need to understand the material well enough to answer any question. Define every term for 2 marks each. Explain the Oedipus/Electra complex for 6 marks. Then write an evaluation of Freud.

Two studies in detail

The two studies given here include Little Hans (which you need to know about) and Axline's study (1964) of a little boy she called Dibs. You may have looked at either Cramer's study (1997) or Bachrach et al.'s meta-analysis instead of the Axline case study.

You will have learned studies by noting the aim(s), procedure(s), results and conclusion(s), which is how they are generally to be described if an exam question asks for the whole study. However, with case study research methods it is hard to separate the procedure(s) from the results and conclusions, so use a different format. For case studies, such as Little Hans and the Dibs study, use aim(s), case background, case description and case analysis (involves conclusions) to make sure that if you are asked a general question you cover enough of the different parts of the study.

Freud's case study of Little Hans (1909)

Aims
One aim was for Freud to follow the development of a young child in order to gather evidence for his ideas or amend his ideas. Another aim was to help with a phobia of horses that Hans (not his real name) had developed.

Case background
Data came from Hans's father, who sent letters to Freud, and Hans sent messages to the 'Doctor' by means of his father's letters. From the information Freud received he analysed Hans's dreams and what Hans said. Freud also analysed the circumstances of Hans's phobia of horses and how it seemed to have developed (as well as how it could be overcome). Freud says that he was careful to use only information from Hans rather than interpretation from the parents.

Case description
The published study is very long and it is best to try to remember just some of the detail; only a few themes are outlined here. Little Hans's father was away a lot and the child seemed to want his father to stay away. It appears that he wanted his father dead, which is a feature that Freud saw as significant. Hans had an anxiety that horses would bite him, and this became a phobia because it affected his behaviour — for example, he would not go out into the street. He said he was afraid that a horse would come into his room and that he was afraid of white horses with black things on their mouths and things over their eyes. He had a dream about giraffes, in which one was

crumpled and Little Hans sat on it, with the other giraffe standing to one side. He also dreamt about what Freud called 'widdlers'. There was a time when Hans was playing at 'having children' using dolls. He said mummy was the children's mummy, Hans was the daddy and Hans's father was the grandfather.

Case analysis

Freud thought that Hans wanted his father dead so that he could take his father's place with his mother. Hans seems to have slept in his mother's bed when his father was away. The fear of the horses, particularly the black things on their mouths and the things round their eyes, was interpreted by Freud as being Little Hans's fear of his father, who had a moustache and wore glasses. The giraffe dream was thought by Freud to be the sex scene, again with Hans dreaming of taking part. All this information was taken by Freud as evidence for the Oedipus complex, where Hans wanted his mother and feared his father. When Hans 'became' the father when playing with the dolls, Freud saw this as resolution of the Oedipus complex and said Hans would then get over his phobia of horses.

Conclusions

Freud followed Hans's progress through the psychosexual stages and used the case study as evidence for the stages, such as the onset of the Oedipus complex and its resolution. The dreams were used to uncover unconscious wishes, and symbols in the dreams were analysed, as in the giraffe dream. Freud thought they provided evidence that dreams are 'the royal road to the unconscious'.

Strengths and weaknesses of the Little Hans study

Strengths	Weaknesses
• The study has much detail and can be re-analysed; it is an in-depth study using qualitative data, which suggests validity • No other method could have gathered the data	• The parents would have been attuned to certain things that Little Hans said and did because they were aware of Freud's theories; Freud would also be looking for certain things, so there is likely to be some subjectivity in interpretation • There are other possible interpretations of the data, such as attachment theory (Hans would be concerned that his mother would leave him) and learning theory (the phobia of horses may have been learned) • The concepts are not measurable so it is not scientific

Axline's case study of Dibs (1964)

Aim

Axline was a clinical psychologist who used play therapy to help Dibs, and her aim was to help him to fulfil his potential, interact with others and 'unlock' problems.

Case background

Axline was called in by the school as a clinical psychologist to help Dibs because, although he appeared to have learning difficulties, the school suspected that in fact he was very bright and could read well. The main part of the study was Axline's story of her sessions with Dibs, including meeting his parents. She quotes Dibs and gives a great deal of detail about what happened in the sessions. She does not provide an analysis of Dibs using psychoanalytic concepts.

Case description

The case study is of 5-year-old Dibs, who lived with a younger sister and his parents, who were clever professional people. They had not wanted children and seem to have found Dibs hard to deal with. Dibs's behaviour was difficult for both the parents and the school, because he spoke rarely and was uncooperative. Problems included that he did not want to go home from school, did not interact with the other children, hid under desks, would not speak and did not join in with activities. But Axline soon found out that Dibs's speech and his writing and reading abilities were well above average.

Her strategy was to ask for Dibs to be brought to her once a week by his parents so that he could play and speak freely; she did not guide him at all. This was play therapy. When speaking to him she reflected back what he said, to let him make his own decisions. She did not put pressure on him by asking questions and she tried not to interpret what he was saying and doing, so that everything came from him.

Axline spoke to his parents a little and found out that his mother had been testing him from a very young age, apparently to make sure there was nothing wrong with him. The mother expected him to get everything right. His father seemed not to love him; he would tell him not to be stupid and criticise him. Axline used the parents' evidence and also evidence from the play therapy. For example, Dibs would use toy soldiers, one of which he called 'Papa'. On one occasion he locked the 'Papa' soldier away. He talked a lot about not liking locked walls and doors, and it seemed as if he had been locked in his room.

Case analysis

Axline makes comments in the case study but does not relate the study to the psycho-dynamic approach specifically. She avoided interpretation during the therapy in order to get 'objective' data. However, it seems as if Dibs worked through his anger, using play and using symbols such as the 'Papa' soldier.

This links to Freud's ideas about fixation and unconscious feelings, which can be released and understood through the use of symbols. Dibs's behaviour in school and at home before the therapy could have come from the id's demands: because the superego had become over-controlling through his parents' expectations, the id's desires had been repressed and needed to be released. Axline's strategy not to ask questions and to let Dibs play freely would have been successful in allowing Dibs's personality to guide him, to get a better balance between the id, ego and superego. Her case study was called 'Dibs in search of self', which suggests her focus was on his personality and achieving a balance.

As Dibs was 5 years old and showed a tendency to want to get rid of his father (evidence coming from his play with the 'Papa' soldier), this can be linked to the

Oedipus complex and a desire to possess his mother, with the related fear of his father. However, Axline does not refer to the Oedipus complex in her analysis.

Conclusions

The case study of Dibs shows how there can be problems if the three parts of the personality are not balanced. It also shows that if problems are acted out, for example through play therapy, they can be released and a balance achieved.

Strengths and weaknesses of the study of Dibs by Axline (1964)

Strengths	Weaknesses
• Qualitative, detailed, rich, in-depth data, including Dibs's actual words, are provided • Uses many different methods (e.g. interviews, observations and play therapy) so there is an opportunity to test for validity	• Difficult to test for reliability as Dibs will never be the same again, so the study cannot be repeated • It is difficult to apply theory to the study, although there are links to psychodynamic theory (e.g. the role of the unconscious, the need to allow catharsis and the appropriateness of the id/ego/superego model of personality)

Exam preparation Make sure you can describe and evaluate each of the two studies (for about 5 marks for description and 5 for evaluation). Or you might be asked to write about the two studies in an essay for 12 marks. Or you might be asked about specific parts of the study, so prepare enough to write about each element: the aim for 2 marks, the procedure, case analysis (4 or 5 marks each), etc.

One key issue

You have to know one key issue that you can explain using concepts and ideas from the psychodynamic approach, so you need to be able to apply what you have learned for the approach to explain real-life issues. You can choose any key issue to study, or indeed more than one. The issue chosen here is about false memories and repression; but if you have studied a different issue, you might prefer to use that.

The debate about false memory and repression

The debate is whether, when undergoing analysis, a person agrees to an interpretation about their life that involves a false memory. The debate is about the power of the analyst and the 'suggestibility' of the analysand (the person undergoing analysis). A memory can be false because it is suggested by the analyst and agreed with but still not true. Alternatively the memory can be true but newly remembered, because during analysis unconscious memories can be uncovered though previously repressed.

Using concepts from the psychodynamic approach to explain the debate

If the memory is true and has been repressed in the unconscious but analysis has revealed the memory, this shows psychodynamic principles at work, such as repression as a defence mechanism and the unconscious as a powerful feature of the mind. If the memory is false, this goes against such psychodynamic explanations: it suggests that analysis can involve implanting false memories and can therefore be undesirable.

Using psychodynamic explanations, it would be argued that the reason traumatic memories are not known before analysis is because they are hidden by the ego to help the personality to gain a balance. The ego uses defence mechanisms, including repression but also denial, projection and displacement. Such mechanisms are likely to lead to traumatic events being 'forgotten', which fits with the idea that 'false' memories are not false but buried. However, there are cases where it is known that the memories were false, such as the case of Beth Rutherford, who 'remembered' abuse by her father and having had an abortion, whereas this could not have been true.

Masson suggested that a problem with psychoanalysis is the power given to the analyst, which can be abused, and this issue is given as a criticism of the approach. However, even when false memories have been 'remembered', it is not thought that they were deliberately implanted. One problem with the psychodynamic approach is that its elements, such as the unconscious, cannot be tested, so there cannot be scientific evidence. The debate about false memories highlights this problem with the approach, as such issues cannot be tested.

Exam preparation Prepare enough discussion about your chosen issue for about 6 marks. Make sure that you can describe the issue without including elements of the psychodynamic approach, because these are needed to explain the issue. Include a criticism of the approach, as an evaluation point can gain a mark.

Practical

You will have carried out a practical within psychodynamic psychology using self-report data and rating scales and leading to correlation data. Go back over your notes to revise what you did, as it is not possible here to help you to revise that part of the course.

Some general ideas about the practical and what to learn

- Make sure you can define the terms 'self-report data', 'rating scale' and 'correlation'.
- Give your aim and the hypothesis, saying whether it is directional or not.
- Be clear about the two rating scales you used.
- Be clear about why you asked your questions and how you gathered the data.
- Understand the sampling method you used (and why).
- Understand how you dealt with ethical issues and/or how some ethical issues were not addressed and why.
- Review how you analysed the data, including using ranking, a scattergraph and a Spearman test. Refer to the learning approach for more about testing and the Spearman test (pp. 53–55).

- Prepare material evaluating a correlational analysis, so that you can evaluate your own study.
- Revise how to write up a study, including knowing about the procedure, sample, apparatus and results, as those are the features your course focuses on for the psychodynamic approach.

Exam preparation Turn the above bullet points into questions and answer them, as you are likely to be asked about them. For example, 'Outline the aim of your practical and state the hypothesis for 2 marks each, and consider two ethical issues you addressed.'

The biological approach

Summary of the biological approach

Definition and key terms

The approach is defined in this section, and key terms are listed and defined in the Content section.

Methodology

This section covers twin and adoption studies, as well as PET and MRI scanning techniques. Various terms regarding experiments and inferential testing are covered. The focus in this approach is on the strengths and weaknesses of using animals in laboratory experiments and the evaluation of experiments in general.

Content

The content includes how neurotransmitters work in the brain, the role of genes in behaviour, including studying the nature–nurture debate, and how the biological approach explains gender behaviour.

Two studies in detail

This section looks at Money (1975), which is the set study for this approach, and Raine et al. (1997), the one chosen from the other studies. You may have covered Gottesman and Shields (1966) or de Bellis et al. (2001) rather than Raine et al.

Key issue

The key issue chosen is the debate over whether autism is an extreme male brain condition; you may have focused on a different key issue.

Practical

You will have carried out at least one practical within the biological approach and you should use your own practical. Some ideas about the practical are suggested in this book.

Definition and key terms

The biological approach is about the influence of genes and the nervous system on behaviour and on how an individual develops. In the content section you will learn about genes, hormones and neuronal transmission.

> **Exam preparation** Define the biological approach, including two examples, for 6 marks. The underpinning ideas that can be used as examples include genes being a key focus for understanding people, and similarly hormones and how the central nervous system works using neurotransmitters. (These issues are explained in the content section for this approach.)

Key terms

The key terms for the biological approach are **central nervous system (CNS)**, **synapse**, **receptor**, **neurone**, **neurotransmitter**, **genes**, **hormones** and **brain lateralisation**. These are all explained in the content section for this approach.

> **Exam preparation** Define each key term for 3 marks, including one example each time.

Methodology

Some of the research methods and methodology used in the biological approach have already been explained in the sections on methodology and on the psychodynamic approach. Those issues are listed below to remind you to revise them.

- experimental hypothesis
- dependent variable (DV)
- credibility
- controls
- reliability
- sampling
- volunteer sampling
- opportunity sampling
- alternative hypothesis
- independent variable (IV)
- ethical issues and humans
- validity
- generalisability
- random sampling
- stratified sampling

> **Exam preparation** List the terms and define them all to check that you fully understand them. Give an example of each where possible and use the biological approach for each example.

Twin and adoption studies

You need to be able to describe twin and adoption studies as research methods and also to evaluate them.

Twin studies

Twin studies are of two types of twins. There are monozygotic (MZ) twins, who are identical, sharing 100% of their genes as they both come from the same fertilised egg. And there are dizygotic (DZ) twins, who are not identical as they come from two eggs that are fertilised at the same time. They share 50% of their genes and can be different genders.

If a particular characteristic comes from genes, then MZ twins, who share all their genes, should share that characteristic. DZ twins should not necessarily share the characteristic as frequently, as they share only 50% of their genes.

So characteristics such as intelligence, schizophrenia, alcoholism, personality and depression are looked at using twin studies. This means looking at the characteristic in twins and seeing if MZ twins share it more frequently than DZ twins. Gottesman and Shields (1966), one of the studies suggested for your course, found that MZ twins share schizophrenia more than DZ twins. So it is thought that schizophrenia is genetic at least to an extent.

Strengths and weaknesses of twin studies

Strengths	Weaknesses
• There is no other way to study genetic influences so clearly because only MZ twins have 100% of their DNA in common	• MZ twins have identical DNA, but epigenetic modification has to be taken into account and they may grow and develop differently because of environmental influences
• MZ twins and DZ twins share their environments, so there is a natural control over environmental effects	• MZ twins may be treated more alike than DZ twins because they are the same sex and look identical; so their environments may not be as controlled as might be thought

Adoption studies

Adoption studies involve looking at children who are adopted and comparing their characteristics with those of their biological and adoptive parents. If an adopted child of a biological mother with schizophrenia, for example, develops schizophrenia when nobody in the family adopting the child has schizophrenia, it might be thought that schizophrenia comes through genes. Studies have found this to be true. You will study schizophrenia at A2.

Strengths and weaknesses of adoption studies

Strengths	Weaknesses
• They control for environment because the children do not share the environment with their biological parent; therefore, similarities with biological parents are genetic	• Families that adopt are similar to each other, so there may be something in that similarity that is causing the results
• Studies can be longitudinal, so developmental trends can be studied	• Families that adopt tend to be chosen to be as similar as possible to the biological families, so the environment may not be very different

Exam preparation   Describe both twin studies and adoption studies for 6 marks each. Then write evaluation points for both research methods, for at least 4 marks each.

PET and MRI scanning techniques

You don't need to evaluate PET and MRI scanning but you do need to be able to describe these research methods.

PET scanning

Positron emission tomography (PET) scanning involves producing computer-generated pictures of the brain. A tracer is taken into the body that emits radioactivity. This can be picked up and formed into a picture of the amount of tracer absorbed, which can indicate which area of the brain/body is functioning. The PET scan measures blood flow and oxygen use.

MRI scanning

Magnetic resonance imaging (MRI) is a scanning technique that uses magnetic and radio waves. The person lies in a large cylinder magnet and radio waves are then sent through the body, affecting the body's atoms. The scanner picks up signals as the atoms move back into position, and the computer turns the signals into a picture.

> **Exam preparation**   You need to be able to describe both of these scanning techniques.

Inferential testing

Inferential testing is considered here for the first time in this book. You need to know about testing using a Spearman test, a Mann Whitney U test and a Chi-squared test. Inferential testing is explained within the learning approach once you have covered the three tests you need to focus on. Therefore, some methodology features that you need for the biological approach are explained in the learning approach. Questions and answers are also given in the learning approach section. The list below shows those terms and issues that you need to know about.

- one- or two-tailed
- levels of significance
- observed value
- evaluation of laboratory experiments
- null hypothesis
- levels of measurement
- critical value

> **Exam preparation**   Write out the terms in the list above and define them all to check that you understand them fully. Refer to the learning approach methodology section for explanations if you need them.

Features of experiments not explained elsewhere

There are just two issues about methodology that need to be explained here. The study by Raine et al. (1997) is an example of using control groups. The other issue is randomising to allocate people to groups and conditions.

Control groups

A control group is a group that is not given any particular task or is not part of the main condition. Control groups give a baseline figure to show what a 'normal' score is, for example. Raine et al.'s (1997) study included a control group and is described in the 'Studies in detail' section for this approach.

Randomising to allocate participants to groups and conditions

In some studies participants are divided between two or more groups. For example, in a memory study when half the participants had to learn letters and the other half had to learn numbers to see if there was a difference, the participants would have to be put into one of the two groups. Participants can be randomly allocated to groups by, for example, tossing a coin for each participant (e.g. tails: they learn numbers; heads: they learn letters). This should help to avoid bias. Or they can be allocated to groups by giving them a number 1 or a number 2 as they arrive. These are just two of various ways of allocating participants to groups.

> **Exam preparation** Explain what a control group is and how participants can be allocated to groups (3 marks each). Include an example in each case, as that can get 1 mark.

Mann Whitney U test

You need to carry out a Mann Whitney U test for your practical. The Mann Whitney U test is used when the design is independent groups and the study is looking for a difference in scores between groups, not a correlation. The data must be more than nominal; levels of measurement are explained in the methodology section of the learning approach. More information about the Mann Whitney U test (and the Spearman test used in the psychodynamic approach) is also found there.

Using animals in laboratory experiments

You need to give examples of using animals in laboratory experiments within the biological approach. Some of these studies are explained in the content section that follows. Make sure you know at least two to describe and evaluate. One way of evaluating the use of animals in laboratory experiments is to consider ethical issues, practical issues and issues of credibility; these are considered below. You can also comment on general issues with laboratory experiments, such as their controls and objectivity making them scientific (which is a strength). Strengths and weaknesses of laboratory experiments are considered in Unit 1 and have issues such as validity, reliability, subjectivity and objectivity, which are reviewed earlier in this book.

> **Exam preparation** Be ready to describe how animals are used in experiments in the biological approach. Material on this follows in the content section.

Ethics, practical issues and credibility with regard to using animals in experiments

Practical issues with using animals

Animals are useful in experiments in psychology for practical reasons, some of which are summarised here:

- Animals can be relatively small and easy to handle.
- Some have relatively short gestation periods and reproductive cycles.

- Some (e.g. mice) have a similar brain structure to humans.
- Some, such as rats, have a short lifespan (2 years).
- Some procedures have to be carried out daily.
- Some procedures require accessing specific parts of the brain that might then be damaged.
- Some procedures require strict control over the environment.

However, there are also practical reasons why the use of animals in experiments can be criticised. Some reasons for not using them are given here:
- Their brains are not going to be identical to human brains.
- Their genetic structures are not the same.
- Human lives are complex and factors rarely occur in isolation.
- For such reasons as these, using animals may not be credible.

Exam preparation Write an essay describing the use of animals in experiments in the biological approach and evaluating practical issues regarding the use of animals in this way. In your answer look at practical reasons for using animals and practical reasons against using animals.

Ethical issues with using animals

There are ethical reasons for using animals in experiments and ethical reasons for not using animals in experiments. The ethical reasons for using animals are summarised here:
- Procedures can be carried out that cannot be carried out on humans and this benefits humans. For example:
  - ablation: removing parts of the brain to see what happens
  - lesioning: damaging parts of the brain to see what happens
- Pro-speciesism suggests that we ought to do all we can to protect our own species.
- Drugs have been developed that could not otherwise have been developed, including drugs for mental health issues.
- The knowledge obtained can improve the lives of the animal species in question.

There are ethical guidelines for using animals in research in psychology, including using animals in experiments. These include the following important rules from the Society for Neuroscience Guidelines for Animal Research:
- Researchers must have a Home Office licence and certificates.
- Anaesthetics must be used appropriately by someone who knows about them.
- Caging and social environment must suit the species.
- Animals must not be subjected to avoidable stress or discomfort.
- Anaesthetic must be given if possible when surgical procedures are involved.
- No more animals must be used than necessary.
- Living animals should only be used when necessary.
- Alternatives should always be sought.
- Research animals must be acquired and cared for according to National Institute of Health (NIH) guidelines.

- There should be reasonable time between experiments so animals can recover and rest.

There are also ethical reasons for not using animals in experiments in psychology, some of which are listed below.

- Many animals feel pain.
- Animals in experiments are not in their natural surroundings and are in unfamiliar, and therefore distressing, conditions.
- Animals should be treated ethically; they are not sufficiently different from humans to be treated as objects.

> **Exam preparation** Prepare an answer about ethical guidelines for animals, and include the negative ethical issues with using animals as well as positive ethical reasons.

Credibility and using animals

There are two aspects of credibility. One is the subjective aspect, of whether we think the data make sense, i.e. whether it makes sense to draw conclusions from animals to humans. The other is the objective aspect, of how strong the data are in respect of how good the methodology is.

From the point of view of a subjective feeling, using animals can be seen as lacking credibility because people are likely to think that animals are too different to humans for results from them to be applicable. However, from the objectivity point of view, using animals is scientific because there can be controls and studies can be repeated to make sure findings are reliable.

> **Exam preparation** Evaluate the use of animals in experiments and discuss issues of credibility.

> **Exam preparation** For the methodology section of the biological approach you need to be able to describe and evaluate laboratory experiments with regard to validity, reliability and generalisability, so make sure you can do that. Material relating to those issues is given at the start of the section on the psychodynamic approach and will be addressed in the learning approach.

Content

You need to know about the role of the central nervous system and how neurotransmitters work in the brain. You also need to know about genes, including the nature–nurture debate; and you need to know specifically how the biological approach explains gender development (including looking at genes, hormones and brain lateralisation). Finally you need to compare biological explanations for gender development with the explanations of the psychodynamic and learning approaches. This final element of the biological approach is covered at the end of the learning approach content section.

The role of the central nervous system and neurotransmitters in human behaviour

The central nervous system (CNS) consists of the brain and spinal cord. The brain guides human behaviour through neurotransmitter functioning. There are many different structures in the brain that have different purposes, but here the focus is on how neurotransmitters work.

Neurotransmitters and messages sent via the synaptic gap

Neurotransmitters such as dopamine and noradrenaline are chemical messengers that travel in the brain between neurones. How this occurs is shown in Figure 2.

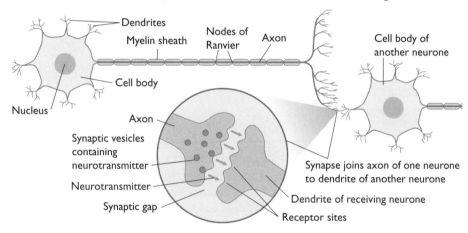

Figure 2 How synapses work

Figure 2 shows the features of neurotransmitter functioning that you need to know about.
- Each neurone has a cell body.
- From the cell body an axon leads down to terminal buttons that hold neurotransmitters in synaptic vesicles and from the cell body there are also dendrites on the end of which are receptors.
- The dendrites of one neurone are close to the terminal buttons of another neurone but in between there is a synaptic gap.
- An electrical impulse travels down the axon and releases the neurotransmitter into the gap.
- The receptors on the dendrites of the nearby cell either receive the neurotransmitter (a chemical) if it 'fits', or they don't if it does not 'fit'.
- If the neurotransmitter is not taken up by the nearby cell the message is stopped.
- If the neurotransmitter is taken up it will trigger an electrical impulse in the cell body, which then travels down that neurone's axon so that the message continues.

Exam preparation Define the following key terms for 2 marks each: neurone, synapse, receptor, neurotransmitter and central nervous system.

The role of genes in behaviour

You need to know about the role of genes in behaviour and also how genes affect gender development, so it makes sense to revise these two parts of your course together.

The nature–nurture debate

Each individual has a genotype, which is the blueprint that is their genetic make-up. Everyone also has a phenotype, which is what the person develops into through their innate genetic make-up interacting with the environment they encounter. Genes are inherited, 50% of them from each of our parents.

A person has their 'nature', which is given by their genes, and their 'nurture', which is given by their experiences with the environment. In the learning approach you will learn more about nurture, so you will be able to discuss the nature–nurture debate more fully later.

What is a 'gene'?

A gene consists of a long strand of DNA (deoxyribonucleic acid); a chromosome is a double chain of DNA. DNA controls gene activity.

> **Exam preparation**   'Gene' is a key term for the biological approach; define it for 2 marks.

The genome is all the genes in a cell; the human genome has around 20 000 genes. There are millions of combinations of the base pairs in DNA that are carried on the 23 pairs of chromosomes that are in each human cell. Genes can, therefore, produce many differences in individuals. The only cells where there are not 23 pairs of chromosomes are the egg and sperm cells, which each have only one strand of 23 chromosomes. When a sperm cell fertilises an egg, their two single strands combine to make 23 pairs, and this is a new life.

Genes and sex differentiation/gender development

Gender is the term usually used when referring to the interaction of the different sexes with the environment, including social norms and rules about gender. Sex is the biological term for male or female.

The sperm cell and the egg cell each have 23 unpaired chromosomes. When the egg is fertilised the two unpaired chromosomes pair up to form a new life, which has 23 unique pairs of chromosomes. This explains why we say that 50% of a person's genes come from their mother and 50% from their father. All brothers and sisters, including DZ twins, share 50% of their genes. MZ twins come from one fertilised egg so they share 100% of their genes.

A male baby (XY) receives an X chromosome from his mother and a Y chromosome from his father. A female baby (XX) receives an X chromosome from her mother and an X chromosome from her father.

From the start an embryo generates hormones, and genes start organising the brain in a gendered way. The way hormones affect gender development is explained below, as is the way the brain differs between males and females. However, for the first 6 weeks or so the embryo develops in the same way whether XX or XY. It is only after that time that sex features start to differ.

Sex differentiation goes through four main steps:
- Fertilisation determines the genetic sex (XX is female and XY is male).
- The fertilised egg divides into identical cells and during development these cells start forming the body organs including the sex organs. The embryo has a gonadal ridge and by about 6 weeks there are two sets of internal ducts. There are the Mullerian (female) ducts and the Wolffian (male) ducts. External genitalia look female.
- The gonadal ridge changes. In males it develops into testes because of a product from a gene on the Y chromosome. In females there is no Y chromosome and other genes form the gonadal ridge into ovaries.
- Hormones then start affecting how the fetus develops, as explained below.

Exam preparation Write an essay about genes and their role in development. Include evidence and examples. (Biological evidence cannot easily be evaluated.)

Hormones as messengers

Like neurotransmitters, hormones carry messages, but not in the same way. Though both involve chemicals, hormones carry messages more slowly. They travel in the blood stream, whereas neurotransmitters are in neurones. Hormones are produced by endocrine glands, which are groups of cells, and affect growth and other processes such as metabolism. 'Female' hormones are oestrogen and progesterone and 'male' hormones are androgens such as testosterone.

Exam preparation 'Hormones' is a key term for this approach; define it for 2 marks.

Hormones and sex differentiation/gender development

From about 6 weeks of gestation the embryo is affected by hormones that govern sex differentiation. For the male fetus (XY) Mullerian (female) inhibiting substance (MIS) stops the growth of the female Mullerian ducts, and androgens (male hormones) affect the growth of the Wolffian ducts. The Wolffian ducts do not grow when ovaries develop in the female fetus (XX) and MIS is not produced then either. MIS stops female growth and androgens lead to male growth. If there are no androgens the embryo remains female.

Evidence for the effects of hormones

In one study hormones were removed from adult female rats so that no oestrogens would be produced. Then the rats were given a form of oestrogen. It was found that low levels of the hormone improved working memory (short-term memory) and high levels impaired memory. This is an animal study so it is useful for you when describing the use of animals in experiments. The study suggests that hormones have a strong effect on behaviour, not only in sex differentiation but in other areas such as memory. Genes dictate the production of hormones, so although for your course the effects of genes on sex differentiation and the effects of hormones have been studied separately, they are connected.

Brain lateralisation

Studies have looked for brain differences between males and females, and differences have been found. One difference is in brain lateralisation, meaning how the two halves of the brain are used. 'Lateralisation' is to do with taking sides, e.g. 'bilateral' means two-sided and 'unilateral' means one-sided. The brain is divided into two hemispheres which are joined by the corpus callosum. It is thought that the left half controls language and the right is concerned with visuospatial ability and perception.

Exam preparation 'Brain lateralisation' is a key term for this approach; define it for 2 marks.

Brain lateralisation and sex differences/gender development

In general it is said that males use the right side of the brain more than they use both sides, while females tend more to use both sides. The corpus callosum — the bundle of fibres connecting the two halves — is larger in women. Evidence for these findings comes from scanning among other techniques.

If men are more lateralised and use the right side more, then they should be better at visuospatial tasks, which it seems they are. Women should be better at language tasks if they use the left side of the brain more than men (in using both sides). You might have carried out a practical looking at these issues. For example, if you gave participants lists of anagrams to solve (e.g. pluper, ngorae and engre put into colour words: purple, orange and green) then female participants should solve more in the time than male participants.

Evidence for brain lateralisation differences
- Studies show that if a male has brain damage in the right hemisphere visuospatial tasks are affected, which supports the idea of gender differences. Studies also show that if males have left-side damage their language abilities are affected. However, it is not found that if females have damage to one side of the brain in this way their skills are similarly affected.
- Men who do not have normal exposure to androgens in the womb tend to use both sides of the brain more.
- High levels of testosterone tend to mean slower neurone growth in the left half of the brain — this study used rats. This would support males using the right half more.

Animal studies

Useful examples of animal studies:

- A study was outlined above where hormones were removed from adult female rats so that no oestrogens would be produced.
- Another study just outlined showed that if rats were given high levels of testosterone they tended to show slower neurone growth in the left half of the brain.

> **Exam preparation** The methodology section gave information on how to evaluate the use of animals in experiments within the biological approach. You need to be able to describe such experiments as well. Use the studies outlined to prepare descriptions of animal experiments within this approach, or use other studies you have looked at.

Evaluation of the biological explanations for gender development

As part of the evaluation of biological explanations for gender development you have to compare those explanations with explanations from the psychodynamic and learning approaches. Such comparisons are reviewed in this guide when you have covered the explanations of the learning approach. In this section, the biological explanations for gender development are evaluated but not compared.

Strengths and weaknesses of biological explanations for gender development

Strengths	Weaknesses
• There is reliability because the studies are replicable and are replicated; measures (e.g. injecting rats with testosterone or using MRI scanning in humans to measure blood flow) are objective • There is validity because different studies using different research methods have similar findings (e.g. such sex differences in brain lateralisation)	• There is a problem with generalisability because many findings come from animal studies; there are important differences in the human brain, so such findings may not be relevant to humans and may not be credible • Biological aspects are difficult to study without reference to the environment; for example, male and female children are reinforced for different behaviour; this may mean that they use different strategies to do tasks, rather than that they have different brain structures

Two studies in detail

The two studies explained here are Money (1975) and Raine et al. (1997). You may have studied either Gottesman and Shields (1966) or de Bellis et al. (2001) instead of Raine et al.

Money (1975) and David Reimer's story

Money (1975) wrote up the case study of a boy who was brought up as a girl. Long after that the 'girl' made himself known to everyone and explained his side of the story. He was David Reimer and you have to know his story as well as the one Money told. The Money case study is outlined here first.

Aims

Money wanted to find out about sex reassignment (when a child or adult changes sex).

Case background/procedure

Money's study looked at many other cases as well, but it is the special case of an identical twin boy brought up as a girl after a circumcision went wrong that you need to be able to describe and evaluate.

Case description

When they were 7 months old a pair of identical twin boys underwent circumcision and one of the operations went wrong. The baby's penis was burnt off accidentally (it was ablated, which means removed) because the electrical current was too strong. The parents, who were not sure what to do, saw John Money on a television programme talking about sex reassignment. After contacting Money and talking with him, the parents chose to bring that son up as a girl. They treated the baby (who was about 17 months old by this time) as a girl, putting 'her' in dresses, encouraging girl play behaviour and changing 'her' name to Brenda. Hormone replacement therapy and surgery were also used as the child got older. Money saw the parents and Brenda fairly regularly over the 9 years of the case study and all seemed to be progressing well. Data were gathered by interviewing the parents and asking Brenda questions. There were reports that Brenda had tomboy traits such as being physically active, but she seemed to want to do 'girl' things and copied her mother's behaviour rather than her father's. At the end of the study it seemed that Brenda saw herself as a girl, albeit a dominant one.

Case analysis

Money concluded that an XY baby, genetically male, could be successfully brought up as a girl and 'become' a girl, and this evidence was used to show that nurture was stronger than nature. However, the update on the study, after the study was concluded, suggested the opposite, as is seen from David Reimer's story.

David Reimer's story: an update on the Money (1975) study

When Brenda was about 14 'she' was told the whole story and it emerged that she had never been happy as a girl and had always felt unhappy and 'wrong'. David/Brenda's mother attempted suicide and his father turned to alcohol. His brother (Brian) became clinically depressed so the family was under enormous pressure. Brenda became David and underwent surgery, though he was depressed and attempted suicide himself. However, he married and had a job, so he had support. When he was about 30 years old he met a psychologist called Diamond, who published a paper about him showing the problems with Money's conclusions, and the whole story was made public. In 2000 David Reimer published a book about himself. In 2002 his brother died of an overdose of antidepressants, David had marital difficulties and was depressed about his brother and unemployed. He again suffered from depression himself and committed suicide. His story strongly suggests that it is nature that is stronger, not nurture.

Strengths and weaknesses of the study by Money (1975)

Strengths	Weaknesses
• The case study is detailed and longitudinal, so there is validity — the data are qualitative and gathered from more than one source	• The study lasted 9 years, but later the participant revealed that he was not happy as a girl, and he chose to live as a man — so, in fact, there was no validity
• The case study has data from more than one source — observation, information from both parents, Brenda's own contributions — so there is reliability	• It is hard to generalise from a unique case like this; not everyone brought up as a girl, although genetically male, will have the same experiences

Raine et al. (1997)

Aims
Raine et al. (1997) wanted to see if there were brain differences between murderers pleading not guilty by reason of insanity and non-murderers.

General procedures
- In the study there were 41 murderers (or people charged with manslaughter, but called murderers in this study) pleading insanity and 41 non-murderers in a control group.
- 23 had a history of brain damage, six had schizophrenia, three had a history of substance abuse, two had a mood disorder, two had epilepsy, three had some sort of learning disability or were hyperactive, and two had a paranoid personality disorder.
- The control group, therefore, also had these features, to make sure there was a match. None of the participants (in either group) was on medication.
- The study took place at the University of California and PET scans were done to gather evidence for the 'insanity' plea or some other part of their trial.
- This is a matched pairs design.
- The IV is whether a participant is a 'murderer' or not.
- The DV is the various measures of brain activity and brain structure found using PET scanning.

Procedure: the PET scanning
Each participant carried out a practice test. Then they were injected with a trace, after which they completed some more tasks such as recognising a target. After about half an hour of uptake of the trace a PET scan was carried out and images of slices of the brain were produced.

Procedure: measuring the brain areas and activity

Slices were checked for glucose levels. Boxes of the brain rather than slices were also examined and linked scan results to the suggested areas for violence. The glucose levels and the brain pictures of the murderers were compared with those of the controls.

Results

The tasks that the participants did before the scans were compared to make sure there were no differences in ability and so on, and there were none. Some of the results for the study are given here:

- The murderers had lower glucose metabolism in some prefrontal areas (the front of the brain).
- In the temporal lobe (a side of the brain) there were no significant differences between the two groups.
- The murderers had lower glucose metabolism in the corpus callosum (the structure that joins the two halves of the brain).
- The murderers had different levels of activity in the amygdala (an area of the brain linked to aggression).

There were other features of the groups that might have affected results:

- As six murderers were left-handed the researchers looked at handedness, and found that it did not affect the results.
- Those with head injury differed only in that they had lower corpus callosum activity.
- As there were 14 non-white murderers they were compared with white murderers, and no significant differences were found.

Conclusions

It was concluded that the murderers had lower glucose activity levels in some brain areas, such as the corpus callosum. They also had abnormal activity in the amygdala and other areas. This suggests that violence has a biological cause. For example, prefrontal deficits can mean loss of self-control, and murderers had different levels of activity in the prefrontal region of the brain. However, the researchers did not conclude that there were only biological causes for violence, just that there might be a predisposition to violence in some people, depending on environmental triggers.

Strengths and weaknesses of the study by Raine et al. (1997)

Strengths	Weaknesses
• PET scanning is an objective technique and the results can be interpreted by more than one researcher; it is a scientific method and is likely to give reliable findings • Largest sample size (up to 1997) for PET scanning and large enough for useful comparison with the control group and for generalisation to murderers pleading not guilty by reason of insanity	• Hard to generalise beyond murderers pleading not guilty by reason of insanity as there were no violent criminals in the control group • Does not show biological causes for violence because environment can cause brain differences

> **Exam preparation** Describe each study for about 6 marks. Be prepared also to write about specific parts of the study, such as the procedure, in detail. Evaluate the studies, including comparing them with regard to their procedures and findings.

One key issue

You need to know one key issue that you can explain using concepts and ideas from the biological approach. The key issue used here is the debate over whether autism is an extreme male brain condition or whether this is not a useful explanation. There are other key issues and if you have learned a different one you might prefer to revise that.

Autism and the male brain

Around 1999 a theory was put forward by Baron-Cohen that autistic people have extreme male brain tendencies. There is an autistic spectrum, which means that there are different degrees of autism, so it is not easy to be precise about what autism is. The condition is mainly characterised as not being able to empathise with others and finding it hard to show love or emotions. However, those with autism often have a high ability with regard to systems and making sense of the world. Males are supposed to be good at systems and not so good at empathy (as in reading emotions from faces). There are more males with autism than females: figures are often quoted as four males to every female. However, there are other explanations for autism as well as it being an extreme level of male brain functioning. For example, Baron-Cohen has put forward another theory and suggested that autism is 'mindblindness' — problems with theory of mind and understanding the thinking of others.

Concepts and ideas from the biological approach can help to explain the idea that autism is an extreme male brain condition. Studies in brain lateralisation have suggested that males use the right half of the brain more while females more frequently use both sides of the brain. Males are better at visuospatial tasks (right hemisphere) than females but not as good at language tasks (left hemisphere). This fits with the idea, as those with autism are often good at visuospatial tasks, which include systems. Also, those with autism show quick brain growth as babies, and boys' brains grow more quickly than girls', again linking autism and male brains. Baron-Cohen's team found that girls are more empathising and boys more interested (and better at) systems, which again supports the theory. Studies show that women are better at interpreting body language as well; this also supports the idea, though it is not proved that this is a biological tendency. Girls' better understanding of emotions has been linked with less testosterone, whereas boys have more testosterone. This too supports the theory — boys with more testosterone would be worse at emotions, as would girls with more testosterone.

Other theories about autism do not say it is the result of extreme male tendencies, although they do focus on brain differences. There is a nature–nurture issue here: it is hard to show a biological or genetic cause of all cases of autism because nature cannot be separated from nurture when studying such a condition.

Exam preparation Describe both the issue of autism and the explanation, using concepts from the biological approach.

Practical

Within the biological approach you will have carried out a test of difference that used an independent measures design and gathered ordinal or interval data. A test of difference means that it was not a correlation. Independent measures means that different people were in the different conditions. Ordinal data are ranked data (e.g. ratings); and interval data are real mathematical data (measurements). Go back over your notes to revise what you did, as it is not possible here to help you to revise that part of the course.

Some general ideas about the practical and what to learn

- Make sure you can give the aim of your study.
- It is likely that you used a biological feature as an independent variable (IV) such as gender or handedness. Make sure you know what your IV was.
- Make sure you know your dependent variable (DV), which will be the measure(s) you chose, such as how many anagrams each participant could solve in a certain length of time or how quickly participants could do a jigsaw.
- Learn the hypothesis and the null hypothesis (do this for all your practicals).
- You need to know why you did a Mann Whitney U test (see pp. 53–54 in the learning approach), so note that down.
- You will have carried out a Mann Whitney U test and worked out whether your study was 'significant' or not. Revise the level of significance you chose, what this means, whether your null hypothesis was accepted or rejected, and why. This means understanding what is meant by observed and critical values, as well as what is meant by one- and two-tailed with regard to tests (see pp. 54–55 in the learning approach for all these issues).
- The design must be independent groups, so make sure you can explain how your study used independent groups.
- You need to know what controls you put in place and some features of the study that were not controlled, though perhaps should have been.
- Note some ethical issues you addressed — and possibly some areas where you did not address ethical issues sufficiently well.
- Revise what level of measurement your data were (see p. 54 in the learning approach) — they had to be either ordinal or interval data.

- Check what your results were, though you do not need to learn every number.
- Revise how you analysed your results, for example which type of graph you used and why.
- Make sure you can evaluate your own practical, looking at these four issues in particular: validity, reliability, credibility and generalisability.

Exam preparation Turn the above bullet point list into questions and answer them in preparation. For example, 'Evaluate your own practical looking at the issues of validity, reliability, credibility and generalisability.'

The learning approach

Summary of the learning approach

Definition and key terms

The approach is defined in this section, and key terms are listed. The key terms are defined in the Content section.

Methodology

For the learning approach you need to know about observations as a research method. You also need to know about using inferential statistics, and some of what you needed for the biological approach is explained here to avoid repetition.

Content

For the learning approach you need to know about three learning theories — classical and operant conditioning and social learning theory. You need to know about one therapy from either classical or operant conditioning, and about how learning theory can explain gender. Finally, you need to consider the three approaches that you have studied for Unit 2 and how they all explain gender in different ways. You need to be able to compare these different ways, and that is dealt with here.

Two studies in detail

You need to know in detail Bandura, Ross and Ross's (1961) study and one other. The other one chosen is Skinner's study of superstition in pigeons, because it uses animals. You need to know at least one animal study so that you can describe and evaluate the use of animals in experiments and consider ethical issues with regard to humans and animals.

Key issue

The key issue chosen for this approach is the influence of role models on anorexia, because it links well with social learning theory and operant conditioning. You may have studied a different issue.

Practical

You will have carried out at least one observation within the learning approach and you should use your own practical for the exam, because you will have 'learned by doing'. Some ideas about the practical are suggested in this book.

Definition and key terms

The nature–nurture debate used to define the learning approach

The learning approach focuses on nurture, whereas the biological approach focuses on nature. The psychodynamic approach looks at nature when saying that we have structures such as the unconscious, the id and the superego; and at nurture when pointing to the importance of upbringing to avoid fixation in any psychosexual stage. Use these points when discussing the nature–nurture issue.

Effects of conditioning on the organism

The learning approach focuses on the conditioning of behaviour. Classical conditioning is about making associations between stimuli and involuntary reflexive behaviour. Operant conditioning is about shaping voluntary, deliberate behaviour to be 'appropriate' or desired.

Effects of reinforcement on the organism

Another strong feature, of both operant conditioning and social learning theory, is the idea of reinforcement affecting behaviour. Operant conditioning explains that rewarding behaviour (giving positive or negative reinforcement) means a behaviour is likely to be repeated. This idea of reinforcement is included in social learning theory.

Effects of social learning on the organism

Social learning involves observing the behaviour of others and in some circumstances copying it. Role models display behaviour, and it is imitated by those watching if certain conditions apply: if the role model is the same gender as the observer, for example.

The effects of the environment

All three learning theories focus on the effects of the environment on behaviour. Involuntary behaviours are conditioned through what happens in the environment (for example, a stimulus produces a response). Voluntary behaviours are reinforced (or not) through environmental influences. Social learning takes place when someone observes what happens in the environment.

Exam preparation Define the learning approach for 6 marks, and include two examples.

Key terms

For the learning approach the key terms are **classical conditioning**, **operant conditioning** and **social learning**, as well as terms that are found within these three types of learning. The terms for classical conditioning are **extinction** and **spontaneous recovery**, as well as **stimulus** and **response**. The terms for operant conditioning are **positive reinforcement**, **negative reinforcement**, **primary reinforcement**, **secondary reinforcement** and **punishment**. The terms for social learning theory are **imitation**, **modelling**, **observation** and **vicarious reinforcement**. All these terms (16 of them) are explained in the content section for this approach.

> **Exam preparation** Define each key term for 3 marks, including one example for each. This task is likely to be easier once you have revised the content section.

Methodology

The new research method you need to learn for the learning approach is observation, which is explained in this section. All features of inferential statistics are also reviewed here; they have been left until this section rather than some being covered in the biological approach.

You also need to use what you have learnt about laboratory experiments, including experiments with humans and animals and ethical guidelines when using humans as participants. These issues are not repeated here; make sure you have revised them.

Issues about experiments are briefly reviewed at the start of the unit (pp. 13–14) and are covered in more detail in the Unit 1 guide. Issues about using animals are summarised in the biological approach (pp. 36–38) and ethical issues when using human participants are summarised in the psychodynamic approach (pp. 19–20).

Observations

Features of observations are fairly straightforward and are briefly explained here. When the term 'observation' is used here, it refers to naturalistic observations.

Features of naturalistic observation as a research method

	Covert (secret)	**Overt (known about)**
Participant	Observer takes part and the study is not known about.	Observer takes part and the study is known about.
Non-participant	Observer does not take part and the study is not known about.	Observer does not take part and the study is known about.

Strengths and weaknesses of different types of observation

	Strengths	Weaknesses
Covert observations	• Behaviour of the participants is likely to be natural because they are unaware that they are being observed; therefore, there is validity • The observation is easier because the observer can carry out the study without the participants watching what the observer is doing	• They are often not ethical because there is no informed consent; if they are not carried out in a public place, they go against ethical guidelines • The observer cannot be helped by the participants (e.g. to find a suitable place for observation) because the participants are unaware that the study is taking place
Overt observations	• They are ethical because informed consent can be gained and the right to withdraw can be given • Observers can ask for help to set up the study (e.g. where to observe from)	• The participants know that they are being watched so might not act in a natural way. Therefore, there is doubt about validity of the data • It might be difficult to carry out because the observers themselves would be watched to see what they are doing
Participant observations	• There is ecological validity because the observation is in the natural setting, including not having a stranger present • A participant observer is likely to gather valid data because the setting is natural and what occurs is also natural	• The observer may be too involved to record all the data, partly because they cannot step back from the situation and partly because they have another role • They are difficult to replicate because it is not easy to find an observer who is also a member of the group
Non-participant observations	• Non-participant observers are objective. They can stand back from the situation better than participant observers • Non-participant observers can record data more easily than participant observers because they have the time to concentrate • They can use time-sampling when tallying, which might be difficult when participating and observing at the same time	• Non-participant observers are likely to affect the situation just by their presence • Non-participant observers might miss the relevance of some interactions or might misunderstand something, whereas participant observers have the advantage of shared understanding with the participants

	Strengths	Weaknesses
Naturalistic observations	• Observations take place in the natural environment of the participant, so there is ecological validity • They gather much in-depth data and detail, which is difficult using any other research method; data are often qualitative and rich; even when quantitative, the data can be detailed	• There might be subjectivity because the observer has to choose what to observe and what to record • An observation is of one group or individual at one moment in time, so the data are not generalisable to other people at different times

Exam preparation You need to know the terms: participant, non-participant, covert, overt, naturalistic observations. Learn a definition of each term. Think of a few examples of observations that could be done (or have been done) using each methodology, so that you can illustrate your answer if asked to explain what a term means.

Inferential statistics

'Inferential statistics' is the overall term for the tests you have used in Unit 2 to see if the results of your practicals are significant or not. You have to know about three inferential statistical tests for your course (there are others).

Once you have gathered your data in any psychology study you need to analyse the results. You can do that using descriptive statistics — mean, median, mode, range, graphs, for example. However, Unit 2 has shown that you can also use statistical tests to see if your study was significant or not. This section explains issues such as 'significant or not' to help you with your revision. It covers the information you need about inferential testing, whichever approach that requirement is listed under in your course.

The three inferential tests in your course

The three inferential tests you need to know about are the Spearman, Mann Whitney U and Chi-squared. The table below shows which test is used in which circumstances. Use the table to give reasons for using the test as well as to find out which test to use.

Which test to use?

Test of difference			
	Nominal data only	**Ordinal data (or interval data)**	**Interval data only**
Repeated measures or matched pairs	*Not required for your course*	*Not required for your course*	*Not required for your course*
Independent groups	Chi-squared	Mann Whitney U	*Not required for your course*

Correlation	
Ordinal data (or interval data)	**Interval data only**
Spearman	*Not required for your course*

You can work out from the table that:
- The test for a test of difference, nominal data, independent groups, is the Chi-squared test.
- The test for a test of difference, ordinal or interval data, independent groups, is the Mann Whitney U test.
- The test for a correlation, ordinal or interval data, is the Spearman test.

Exam preparation Make sure that you can choose a test for a study if you are asked to do this in the exam, and that you can give reasons for your choice.

Choosing a level of significance

You have to test how far results are likely to be due to chance. Three levels of significance are summarised here to show you what a level of significance is.

If you accept that 5% of the results or fewer are due to chance, you would usually say the study 'worked' at the 5% level of significance. How you say this is $p \leq 0.05$; this means that the probability of the results being due to chance (p) is equal to or less than ($\leq$) 5% (0.05). 5% is 1 in 20, so you would accept that 1 in 20 of the results is due to chance, while 19 in 20 (95%) are due to what was done in the study.
- 0.10 is 10% being due to chance — not acceptable
- 0.05 is 5% being due to chance — acceptable
- 0.01 is 1% being due to chance — better and more acceptable

Levels of measurement

For your course in psychology there are three levels of measurement:
- nominal = data in categories, such as aggressive or not
- ordinal = data that are ranked, such as rated on a scale of 1 to 5
- interval/ratio = data that are mathematical measurements, such as degrees Celsius or time

Exam preparation Make sure you know about the three levels of measurement and about levels of significance. Questions are likely to be asked using these terms, and it would be a pity to lose marks because you are not sure of the terminology.

Writing a null hypothesis

The hypothesis (the alternative, or experimental, hypothesis) is the statement of what is expected to happen in a study, and the null hypothesis states that it will not happen, because any difference or relationship will be due to chance. It is the null hypothesis that is tested by an inferential test. The test determines how far the results are due to chance rather than what was expected, and therefore whether what was expected has happened or not. An example of a null hypothesis is: 'There is no significant difference between males and females when it comes to what type of car they drive, small or large.'

One- or two-tailed with regard to tests

A hypothesis is directional if it says which way the results will go, for example: 'Males will drive large cars and females will drive small cars.' In testing, directional is called 'one-tailed'.

A hypothesis is non-directional if it does not specify which way the result will go, for example: 'There is a difference in size of car driven depending on whether the driver is male or female.' In testing, non-directional is called 'two-tailed'.

Exam preparation Practise writing out the hypothesis, null hypothesis and whether the hypothesis is directional (one-tailed) or non-directional (two-tailed) for a number of studies that you have either carried out or looked at.

Critical and observed values

The result of doing an inferential test is the observed value. For each type of inferential test there are tables of critical values, against which you can check your observed value to see if your result is significant.

How to compare critical and observed values

- First you need to know your observed value, which comes from working out the test result. In your practical for the psychodynamic approach you will have carried out a Spearman test, which will have given you a result ρ. For the biological approach you will have worked out the result of a Mann Whitney U test, giving you the U value. For the learning approach you will have worked out the result of a Chi-squared test, giving you the Chi-squared value (χ^2).
- Then you need the right critical values table. These tables are found in statistics books or on the internet. Find the right table for each test.
- Then you need to know: for the Spearman test, the number of participants; for the Mann Whitney U test, the number of participants in each group (this will have been an independent groups design); for the Chi-squared test, the degrees of freedom, which for a 2 by 2 table is 1.
- Finally, choose a level of significance of 0.05 (5%) and decide whether your hypothesis is one- or two-tailed.
- Armed with all this information, you will be able to look along the rows and columns of the table and compare your observed value with the critical value to see if the result is significant or not.
- The table will tell you whether your result has to be larger or smaller than the one in the appropriate box of the table.

Exam preparation Find the results of the three tests for your three practicals and check the observed values in each case against the critical value tables to check your understanding. Or just make up some results of the three tests (e.g. $\rho = 0.58$, $U = 8$ and Chi-squared $= 4.72$) and see if these results are significant, given fictitious levels of significance, numbers of participants and other features.

Laboratory experiments using animals and humans

Revise all that you have learned about laboratory experiments, as questions about them can be asked in this unit. The issues are not discussed here as they are found elsewhere in this guide.

Exam preparation Write down four features of laboratory experiments and four evaluation points.

Ethical guidelines for the use of humans in studies

Revise the guidelines for using human participants, which are summarised in this guide in relation to the psychodynamic approach.

> **Exam preparation** Define each of the five main guidelines your course focuses on and think of an example of the use of each.

Content

There are three theories of learning and you have to know about all three of them. You need to know how gender development is explained and one therapy from either classical or operant conditioning.

Classical conditioning

Pavlov is the main person associated with classical conditioning, so an example from his studies is given here.

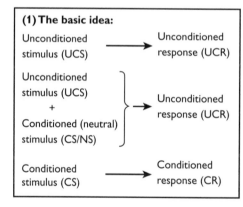
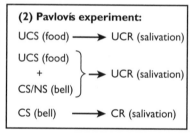

Classical conditioning

> **Exam preparation** Make sure you can fit the main features into a diagram like this if you are given one in the exam (features are UCS, UCR, NS, CS, CR)

Other features of classical conditioning

Extinction occurs when the association (for example, between the bell and the food) is no longer presented. After a while the response (salivation) no longer occurs when the stimulus (the bell) appears.

Spontaneous recovery is the term for when, after extinction, a previously conditioned association (for example, salivating to the sound of a bell) reoccurs without more conditioning. The response to the stimulus reoccurs spontaneously.

> **Exam preparation** Extinction and spontaneous recovery are two of the key terms for this type of learning. Define the terms and give an example of each.

Operant conditioning

Another type of conditioning is operant conditioning. Some features of operant conditioning are given in the table below.

Features of operant conditioning

Feature of operant conditioning	Explanation
Positive reinforcement	Something good is given because of the behaviour, so the behaviour is repeated.
Negative reinforcement	Something bad is taken away because of the behaviour and so the behaviour is repeated.
Punishment	Something bad is given and the behaviour is stopped.
Primary reinforcement	The reward is a basic need, like food or warmth.
Secondary reinforcement	The reward is something that can buy or get a basic need, like money or tokens.

Strengths and weaknesses of operant and classical conditioning theories as explanations of human behaviour

Strengths	Weaknesses
• Studies use experimental method and controls so they are scientific and cause-and-effect conclusions can be drawn • Both can be applied in therapies and so they have practical applications	• Studies use animals, so generalisability and credibility are in doubt • Studies are laboratory experiments and use animals, so validity is in doubt

Exam preparation Classical conditioning, extinction, spontaneous recovery, stimulus and response are key terms; define them and give an example for each. Do the same with operant conditioning, positive reinforcement, negative reinforcement, primary reinforcement, secondary reinforcement and punishment.

One therapy from classical conditioning: systematic desensitisation

You need to study one therapy from classical or operant conditioning; systematic desensitisation is the one chosen here.

Systematic desensitisation is used to cure phobias using principles of classical conditioning. The example of a spider phobia explains the treatment. The aim is to replace the phobia of spiders with a new association, 'lack of fear'. This lack of fear is operationalised (made measurable and useful) as relaxation. The treatment is to desensitise the individual so they are no longer sensitive to (have a phobia of) spiders; and it is systematic because it is in steps.

The first step is to teach the person deep muscle relaxation, so that they can achieve the desired relaxed response. The next step is gradually to introduce the idea of spiders while the person relaxes. Then a picture of a spider is introduced, still with relaxation. The final step is a real spider, with the person being taught to stay relaxed. In this way the person is systematically (step-by-step) desensitised to (taught not to be afraid of) spiders. Other phobias can be treated in the same way.

Strengths and weaknesses of systematic desensitisation

Strengths	Weaknesses
• It is more ethical than other therapies for phobias (e.g. flooding) because it involves a gradual exposure to phobic objects or situations and individuals are involved fully in their therapy	• Not everyone can learn to relax and take such a central part in therapy; it is only useful for some mental health issues, and not, for example, for psychoses
• The therapy has a clear rationale based on classical conditioning that can both explain the phobia or anxiety and also remove it	• There are issues such as operant conditioning principles and cognitive processes being involved, so the explanation — resting on classical conditioning — is not the whole story
• Studies show that the therapy is successful (e.g. Capafons et al. 1998 showed that it helped to overcome a fear of flying)	

Social learning theory

The third learning theory you need to know about is social learning theory. Features of the theory are:

- Children and others learn from role models — people looked up to and identified with.
- Social learning theory is observational learning. The behaviour of role models is observed in particular.
- After the behaviour is observed it is then imitated.
- Social learning theory involves cognitive elements — behaviour is modelled. To be imitated it needs to be observed, attended to, stored in memory and rewarded so that there is motivation to reproduce it.
- Whether the behaviour is repeated depends on various issues such as whether the role model was rewarded for the behaviour, and whether the observer identifies with the model (e.g. being the same gender or similar in some other way).
- Male models are more relevant to boys, and males are more likely to display aggression; therefore boys are more likely to copy aggressive role models.
- 'Vicarious learning' is behaviour that is carried out because of seeing someone else carry it out and seeing them being rewarded for it. 'Vicarious' means not direct.

Strengths and weaknesses of social learning theory as an explanation of human behaviour

Strengths	Weaknesses
• There is a great deal of experimental evidence to support the theory and the behaviour that is learned is visible, so the evidence is strong	• There might be a lack of validity as the behaviour might not be exhibited immediately, so it might be thought that no learning had taken place, when, in fact, it had
• The theory gives rise to practical applications such as in therapy and in explaining, for example, why violence on television or in media games might be copied	• Studies are often carried out on animals and it can be difficult to generalise to humans from animal studies

> **Exam preparation** The key terms within social learning theory are imitation, modelling, observation and vicarious reinforcement. Define each of these terms and give an example.

Learning theories and gender development

You need to be able to explain gender differences and gender development. For example, how are girls and boys different, and what is the explanation for any differences?

How gender can be learnt through 'learning' principles

Learning theory	Gender explanation
Operant conditioning	Gender behaviour is reinforced like other behaviour. For example, boys and girls are rewarded for appropriate behaviour depending on cultural norms. As well as positive reinforcement there is likely to be negative reinforcement and punishment.
Social learning theory	Gender behaviour is shown by role models and imitated like other behaviour. Relevant behaviour is imitated, and it seems that gender is one way of identifying with a model.

Strengths and weaknesses of learning explanations for gender behaviour

Strengths	Weaknesses
• Learning explanations test observable behaviour in experimental conditions and so are developed using objective scientific method • Animal studies show that learning explanations can also explain animal behaviour and that such explanations are reliable	• Learning theory explanations should mean that different cultures exhibit different gender behaviour, but there are developmental sequences that are similar between cultures • In newborn babies, there are gender differences that cannot have been learned, so not all differences in gender behaviour can be explained by learning theories

Comparing the three approaches and their gender explanations

The psychodynamic approach has its own explanation for gender behaviour, maintaining that children at about 5 years old identify with their same-sex parents and display appropriate gender behaviour. The biological approach sees gender more as about sex assignment (giving people a label about their gender according to their genetic make-up). It has three focuses for gender development: genes, hormones and brain differences. It explains that males have XY and females have XX chromosomes. This assignment of chromosomes at conception leads the genes to dictate which hormones will be at work from about 7 weeks after conception. So hormonal activity (which continues throughout the individual's life) differs between the sexes and dictates gender behaviour. Gender differences are also explained by brain differences, such as brain lateralisation, which is different for males and females.

Comparison of the three approaches and explanations for gender behaviour/development

Feature	Psychodynamic approach	Biological approach	Learning approach
Influence of genes	Inherited tendency to Oedipus complex	XX for females and XY for males	Not considered
Influence of environment	Need parents to identify with in phallic stage	External environment (e.g. abuse or neglect) can affect development	Completely responsible for gender behaviour and development — pattern of reinforcements and also role of models such as parents and peers
Influence of neuro-transmitters and hormones	Not considered	Influential; if hormones are not produced or reacted to normally, gender development can be affected strongly	Not considered
Sex assignment	Gender development is focused on more than sex assignment	Sex assignment is the main focus	Gender behaviour is focused on more than sex assignment
Scientific study	No — evidence difficult to find and tends to be qualitative	Yes — laboratory studies, reductionist, scanning and animal studies	Yes — laboratory studies when considering reinforcement; what is measurable is not as clear as in the biological approach
Focus on social norms	Yes — a boy identifies with his father and takes on his norms and values (similarly for girl and mother)	Not considered	Yes — social norms are required and reinforced; modelling (e.g. copying parental behaviour) also leads to following social norms
Concept of identification	Yes — with same-sex parent, but with unique explanation	Not considered	Yes — with role models
Use of case studies	Yes — focuses clearly on case-study evidence	Yes — particularly case studies of abnormal development	Possible — such as of a person who appears to have committed a crime because of modelling — but less likely than in the other two approaches
Use of animal studies	No	Yes — findings from animal studies used to draw conclusions about humans	Yes — when considering reinforcement; less so when looking at social learning

Nature–nurture and gender differences

The three approaches for Unit 2 differ with regard to the nature–nurture debate, as explained under 'Definition and key terms' above.

Exam preparation First, describe how the different learning theories can explain gender-specific behaviour. Then evaluate one or more of those explanations. Finally, compare the three different approaches and their explanations of gender behaviour.

Two studies in detail

The two studies explained in this section are the 'set' study, which is Bandura, Ross and Ross (1961), and one of the other prescribed studies, Skinner (1948). You may have studied Pickens and Thomson (1968) or Little Albert (1920) rather than Skinner; if so, you should consider revising that.

Bandura, Ross and Ross (1961)

Aims

To see whether young children imitate behaviour they have seen. One specific aim was to see if children copy behaviour later whether it is rewarded or not.

Procedure: the sample

The participants were 36 boys and 36 girls aged from about 3 to 5 years old who attended Stanford University nursery. The study, a laboratory study at the university, involved a female role model and a male role model who each displayed aggressive behaviour and non-aggressive behaviour (the two main conditions). There were eight groups of children, four of the groups were all boys and four of the groups all girls. Half the groups (split into boy/girl groups) watched an aggressive model, half a non-aggressive model; within these conditions, half watched the same-gender adult model and half watched the opposite-gender model. There was also a control group of children who did not watch either aggressive or non-aggressive behaviour. Importantly, the participants in the experimental and control groups were matched for aggression before the study started.

Exam preparation Use this study to explain control groups and their purpose and the use of an independent groups design. Studies like this are useful for illustrating methodological issues.

Procedure: how the study was carried out

The children were seated individually in a room with some materials to play with (not the same toys as the adult models had available). In an opposite corner of the room an adult model carried out the planned behaviour. In the aggressive condition the adult behaved aggressively towards a Bobo doll, employing other toys and aggressive language (for example, 'sock him on the nose'). In the non-aggressive condition the adult played calmly and modelled calm, anti-aggressive behaviour. The control group of children did not watch any behaviour, they just sat in the same room and played. Then the child was taken to another room and made to feel slightly aggressive by being told they could not play with certain toys. Finally the child was taken to a different area where the Bobo doll and the toys the adult had used were available. The child was observed. The observers recorded the play behaviour of each child and watched for the acts of the role models (such as the child saying 'sock him on the nose' or hitting the doll with the mallet).

Results

In the non-aggressive condition very little aggressive behaviour was recorded and around 70% of the children showed no aggression at all. In the aggressive condition a lot of the adult's behaviour was seen, including both the verbal and physical aggression. Girls in the non-aggressive condition performed on average 0.5 aggressive acts with the mallet, whereas in the aggressive condition an average of 18 aggressive acts with the mallet were observed in girls. About 13 aggressive acts with the mallet were observed in the girls in the control condition, so it is thought that modelling non-aggressive behaviour leads to less aggression. There were many other findings, such as that in general the boys were more aggressive than the girls, although girls tended to show verbal aggression. It was in physical terms that the girls were less aggressive.

Conclusions

The general conclusions were that a male adult showing aggressive behaviour is copied more than a female adult aggressive model, which perhaps shows cultural differences. Girls tend to be more verbally aggressive than physically aggressive. For aggression with the mallet, the non-aggressive condition led to fewer aggressive acts than in the control group, which perhaps shows that non-aggressive behaviour can lower aggression.

Strengths and weaknesses of the study by Bandura, Ross and Ross (1961)

Strengths	Weaknesses
<ul><li>The study has controls with operationalisation of variables, so cause-and-effect conclusions can be drawn; for example, the aggressive acts were set up so that they could be observed later</li><li>There is reliability because two judges observed the behaviour and their scores could be compared; one judge did not know to which condition a child had been allocated, so was not biased</li></ul>	<ul><li>The situation was not natural; the children might have thought that they were supposed to hit the Bobo doll, given that they had seen adults doing it</li><li>The study might not be ethical because children observed verbal and physical aggressive acts and repeated them; how ethical issues were dealt with was not clearly explained</li></ul>

Skinner (1948)

The second study described here is Skinner's (1948) study of eight pigeons, in which he found what he called superstitious behaviour.

Aims

Skinner's aim was to study operant conditioning to find out more about the effects of rewarding behaviour — positive reinforcement. His specific aim was to see if behaviour that occurred as a reward was given would be repeated because it had been casually reinforced.

Procedure

Eight pigeons were used in this study. Each was put into a cage where there was a food hopper that could be swung in to deliver food pellets to the pigeon. The pigeon's behaviour was filmed in detail and two observers watched carefully. Each pigeon was starved to 75% of its normal body weight to make it hungry enough for the pellets to be a reward. The hopper was periodically swung into place for 5 seconds and taken away again. It is important that the reward was swung in without paying attention to the behaviour of the pigeon. The question was whether the pigeon, having eaten and wanting more, would then reproduce whatever behaviour it happened to be performing at the time, connecting that behaviour with the reward.

Results

The results were clear, with both observers agreeing closely. In six of the eight trials (six of the eight pigeons) the bird exhibited the same behaviour to try to get the reward.

These are the behaviours that were repeated by the eight pigeons:
- One bird turned anticlockwise, making two or three turns before getting the reward.
- One bird pushed its head into the upper corners of the cage.
- One bird did head tossing.
- Two birds carried out a pendulum motion.
- One bird made pecking movements towards the floor.
- Two birds did not show recognisable behaviours.

The six birds that repeated behaviour continued to do so until the reward was received. The shorter the time before the food returned, the more the behaviour was displayed. If a 1-minute interval was used before the food returned, then the bird tended to show different behaviours and then settle on one marked one to repeat, like a sharp movement of the head which became more definite.

Conclusions

The bird behaved as though the behaviour (such as pecking towards the floor) had caused the food to appear. So that behaviour was conditioned. This was called 'superstitious' behaviour because although it had not been deliberately conditioned, the bird behaved as if it had. This is similar to a person who does well in an exam while wearing a favourite jumper attributing the good result to the jumper (to an extent) and wearing it again for the next exam; this is a superstition.

> **Exam preparation** An exam question may ask you to describe a study in detail; do this for each study. Make sure you know enough detail to deal with specific questions about procedure or findings. (Findings include results and/or conclusions.)

One key issue

You can use any key issue to explain using concepts and ideas from the learning approach. The key issue used here is whether those with anorexia copy media role models. There are other key issues and if you have learned a different one you might prefer to revise that.

Role models and anorexia

A common accusation is that thin role models are linked to increasing diagnoses of anorexia, particularly perhaps in girls, but also in boys. The issue is whether such models do cause eating disorders or whether there is another explanation. Sufferers of anorexia regard themselves as fat even when they are dangerously underweight (weight at least 15% lower than it should be). There is a high incidence of anorexia among teenage girls and the rate of anorexia in boys is rising.

Learning theories can help to explain anorexia. Social learning theory suggests that people imitate role models, especially those they see as relevant to themselves. It is likely, therefore, that teenage girls will imitate female models and media celebrities, where there is a trend to be very slim/thin. There are also rewards for being thin through praise and admiration from friends and family. And there is negative reinforcement against being fat, because being fat brings criticism and teasing. To avoid being teased, fat children might starve themselves to slim down and this might turn into anorexia.

However, anorexia could also be explained in a different way. The psychodynamic approach suggests that a girl might starve herself to avoid growing up because she is fixated at a certain psychosexual stage. Nevertheless, cross-cultural studies support the idea of anorexia being learned, because the incidence of anorexia differs in different cultures according to varying social norms.

> **Exam preparation** Write a description of the issue, making sure you are not using psychological explanations. Then give psychological explanations from the learning approach. You could add an alternative explanation as an evaluation point. And you could evaluate the explanation of the issue by evaluating the approach.

Practical

You will have carried out a practical within the learning approach using an observation. Go back over your notes to revise what you did, as it is not possible here to help you to revise that part of the course.

Some general ideas about the practical and what to learn

- Note the hypothesis and null hypothesis for your study.

- Note also the IV and the DV, as well as the sampling method and details about participants.
- Be ready to explain whether your observation was covert, overt, participant or non-participant. If you used a video recording to gather data, remember that it is not a content analysis: you were not analysing the video recording itself and what was chosen to be included in it, you were analysing the data as they were observed.
- Make sure you know about controls you put in place and why. Also think about what was not controlled, and the reasons for this.
- Make sure you know about ethical issues you dealt with, and perhaps also some ethical issues you could not address and the reason for this.
- Make sure you know why you gathered quantitative data (such as by tallying).
- Note why you chose a Chi-squared test (apart from having been told to), the level of significance, the level of measurement, that it was an independent groups design, and whether the test had to be one- or two- tailed (and why). See pp. 53–55 for explanations of this.
- Have a good understanding of how the results and analysis of results were written up (e.g. mean, median, mode, range, graphs).
- Note whether the result of the test (the observed value) was significant or not by checking against the critical values (see p. 55 for explanations of this).
- Be ready to evaluate your study in terms of validity, reliability, generalisability and credibility.

Exam preparation Practise using the above bullet points as questions and prepare answers. For example, 'What controls did you put in place and why?'.

Glossary

This section contains definitions of the key terms that you need to know for Edexcel AS psychology Units 1 and 2. They are organised by unit and subdivided into each approach.

Unit 1

The social approach

Agency theory Milgram's explanation for obedience to those in authority. He thought that being in an agentic state would benefit society and so might be a behaviour that was handed down through natural selection.

Agentic state the state people are in when they are acting as agents for someone else or society rather than acting according to their own principles and their own decisions.

Alternative hypothesis the statement of what is expected in a study, such as 'young females who have just passed their test are better drivers around a prescribed course than young males who have just passed their test'.

Autonomous state the state people are in when they are acting for themselves and making their own decisions, as opposed to being in an agentic state.

Closed-ended (closed) questions questions that ask for specific responses, where the answers are restrained by boxes or categories of replies such as yes/no answers or ratings on a scale.

Cognitive dissonance a theory put forward by Festinger to account for how people change completely when one aspect of them changes. According to the theory, if someone's behaviour is at odds with their emotions and their thinking, that person experiences feelings of discomfort or guilt; so to resolve these feelings, they have to change their emotions and thinking as well.

Confidence interval the plus or minus figure that shows the extent to which you accept that any results are not likely to be true. For example, you might say you have confidence in the findings of your survey within plus or minus 3 of the percentages found, which is a high confidence level.

Confidence level the percentage of a sample that is likely to represent the population. For example, in a survey you might have a confidence level of 95% because not all the answers will truly represent the population: there are always chance factors for some results, such as a misunderstanding of the question or someone guessing.

Controls procedures in a study that make sure that what is done and measured is not affected by external factors such as noise, time of day, temperature, bias from the researcher or anything else. If a study is carefully and well controlled then findings are secure — they are about what they say they are about. Controls are put in place to avoid bias.

Data results and findings from studies of any sort. Data are what are gathered from a study and can be either qualitative or quantitative.

Debrief an explanation given at the end of a study to a participant, saying what the study was about, what results were expected and how the results will be used. It gives the participant the chance to ask questions and the right to withdraw their data.

Deindividuation the idea that people can become unidentifiable as individuals in certain situations, such as when wearing a uniform or when in a crowd. People can then act in ways in which they would not normally act because their control over themselves as individuals is to an extent lost.

Demand characteristic a feature of a study that gives a clue about what is intended, so that a participant can either try to help the researcher by doing what they think is wanted or be unhelpful. Either way data are not valid so the study is not a good one. It is a form of bias.

Discrimination an action arising from a prejudiced attitude.

Ethics principles of right and wrong with regard to the actions of others or of societies, and issues concerning right and wrong. There are ethical guidelines for the treatment of both human and animal participants of studies. Researchers need to make sure that studies with human participants do not upset anyone and that everyone is treated fairly and with respect.

Experimental hypothesis the alternative hypothesis for an experiment (i.e. for any other research method it is called the alternative hypothesis). The experimental hypothesis is the statement of what is expected in an experiment, such as 'more words from a list are recalled if they are learnt in categories than if learnt as a random list'.

Hypothesis the statement of what is expected when a test or study is to be carried out. The alternative or experimental hypothesis says what is expected while the null hypothesis says the opposite — that any results found in a study will not be significant enough to draw conclusions and are likely to be due to chance. Statistical tests look to see if results are significant enough to be unlikely to be due to chance.

Informed consent the agreement of participants to take part in a study on the basis that they know what the study is about, and the principle that they must be given this information before taking part.

In-group the group that someone categorises themselves as belonging to.

Interview a way of collecting data by asking spoken questions. Structured interviews have a set of questions that are stuck to. Semi-structured interviews involve some set questions but some allowance for exploring issues. Unstructured interviews involve an interview schedule or set of questions but then the interviewer can explore different areas that arise according to the respondent's answers.

Interviewee a person being interviewed. The participant in an interview is called the interviewee and the participant in a questionnaire is called the **respondent**.

Likert scale a rating scale that uses categories for gathering data. There might be five points on a scale, for example: 'strongly agree', 'agree', 'unsure', 'disagree', 'strongly disagree'.

Methodology a set of research methods and everything to do with them.

Natural selection according to evolution theory, the passing on of any tendency that aids survival. If an organism with a particular characteristic survives to reproduce, the genes causing that characteristic are passed on.

Null hypothesis the statement that the difference or relationship predicted to happen in a study will not happen. For example, 'young female drivers who have just passed their test will not be better drivers around a prescribed course than young male drivers'. The null hypothesis acknowledges that there might still be a difference in the driving of the two genders but any difference there is will not be large enough to conclude that the difference in driving is because of the difference in gender. The difference could be due to chance or to another factor not considered. A statistical test looks to see if a difference that is found is likely to be due to chance. If the test shows that the difference is large enough for it to be unlikely to be due to chance, then the null hypothesis (which says there is not a large enough difference) will be rejected and the alternative hypothesis (which says there is a difference) will be accepted.

Obedience obeying someone in authority (an authority figure).

Objectivity not allowing personal views to affect analysis, so that findings are relevant, reliable and valid. Science requires objectivity because if factors about a researcher affect results, then the results cannot be used to build a body of knowledge.

Open-ended (open) questions asking for people's opinions and attitudes in a way that allows them to write whatever they like, without being limited in any way.

Opportunity sampling the researcher takes whoever is available to take part in the study. The sample is sometimes called a grab or convenience sample.

Out-group the other group, when someone categorises themselves as being in the in-group. Those in the in-group become prejudiced and discriminate against the out-group.

Participant the person providing the data in a study — the person taking part. The participant used to be called the 'subject' until it was realised that this made them more like an 'object' than an individual with a part in the study.

Personal data information about respondents such as their age, gender, occupation, whether they have a driving licence — whatever is of interest.

Pilot survey a small-scale practice run of a task or survey to find out any problems and put them right before the real thing.

Placebo something pretending to be a substance such as medication when it is actually something else that is harmless, like glucose. It is given so that participants in a study do not know whether or not they are receiving whatever is the subject of the study — or it is given for safety reasons, so that no harm is done.

Prejudice a negative attitude towards someone or a group that results in stereotyping. Prejudice can be positive but is usually negative. Any negative attitude based on uncertain facts is a prejudiced attitude.

Presumptive consent consent to taking part in a study that is assumed to be given even though the actual participants are not fully informed about it. Other people, not the participants, are fully informed and asked if they would take part in such a study; if they would, it is assumed that the actual participants would not mind either.

Prior consent consent to taking part in a study in cases where participants are asked in general if they would be volunteers for a study without knowing exactly what it is about.

Qualitative data opinions and attitudes that are gathered and analysed rather than set answers. In a questionnaire qualitative data are gathered by open-ended questions.

Quantitative data data gathered in the form of numbers, such as numbers of yes/no answers, and measurable categories, such as ratings on a scale of 0 to 10. In a questionnaire quantitative data are gathered by closed-ended questions.

Reliability The extent to which the same (or very similar) data are yielded when a test or study is run again. If data from a repeat of the study are very similar, then the study is said to give reliable results. If they were not reliable, findings from the study could not be added to a scientific body of knowledge.

Representative sample a sample in which everyone in the target population is represented. For example, if the target population includes all females, then females of every age should be part of the sample, and perhaps females with different educational backgrounds and different jobs.

Respondent the person giving the answers in a survey; the participant.

Response bias factors in the question or task giving a bias, such as tending to suggest the answer 'yes' and thereafter getting that answer regardless; or bias in the respondent, such as having the type of personality that tends to agree or disagree. Such a person may try to be helpful, for example, and say what they think is wanted.

Response set either getting into the habit of answering in a particular way (such as 'yes') to a set of questions and so continuing in that way regardless. This can happen if a Likert-type scale is used and all the statements are phrased so that 'strongly agree' is in the same direction (such as being prejudiced). Such statements should be mixed so that sometimes a prejudiced person would answer 'strongly disagree'. A particular type of response bias.

Sampling the way people are chosen to take part in a study. Usually not all the people being studied can be involved, so there has to be a sample.

Sampling frame the people chosen from which the sampling is done. The whole target population cannot usually be chosen, so there is a suitable sampling frame, such as one primary school to represent all primary schools.

Schedule in an interview, the list of questions, any instructions, and any other information such as the length of time for the interview.

Science building a body of knowledge in such a way that others can rely on the knowledge. This involves objectivity, measurable concepts (so that the tests can be done again), careful controls, and the generating of hypotheses from previous theory (so that one piece of evidence can link to another one to build the knowledge).

Self-rating giving a rating score about oneself, such as for attractiveness or meanness.

Simple random sampling a method of sampling by which everyone in the sampling frame or target population has an equal chance of being chosen to be included in the sample.

Social categorisation a process of accepting oneself as being part of an in-group, according to social identity theory.

Social comparison the process of comparing one's in-group with the out-group and thinking of the in-group as better in some way. This enhances the individual's self-esteem and can lead to prejudice.

Social desirability the tendency we have to say what we think we ought to say or do what we ought to do in a given situation. For example, it is socially desirable to say we recycle rubbish so a survey is likely to find that we do — even if we do not — because we are likely to say that we do. It is a form of bias.

Social identification a process of identifying with an in-group after categorising oneself as being part of the in-group.

Stereotyping transferring an opinion about an individual onto other individuals or groups.

Stratified sampling a method of sampling by which the target population is divided into required groups or strata, and corresponding proportions of people from these groups are picked out for the sample.

Subjectivity allowing personal views to affect analysis so that findings are affected.

Surveys interviews and questionnaires in which questions are asked to gather data.

Target population all the people the results will be applied to when the study is done.

Validity the extent to which a test or study yields data that apply to a real-life setting and real-life situations; the extent to which the data are 'true'. If a study is measuring what it claims to measure (for example, if it has really found out about prejudice, and not just what we think we should say about prejudice) then it is said to give valid results. If they were not valid, findings from the study could not be added to a scientific body of knowledge.

Volunteer/self-selected sampling a method of sampling by which people are asked to volunteer for the study either personally or via an advertisement. They self-select themselves by volunteering.

The cognitive approach

Baseline measure a measure of what would 'normally' be the case so that in an experiment a difference can be tested for. It comes from the control group; the researcher compares the control group with the experimental group to see what difference the experiment has made.

Capacity size; in the multi-store model of memory, the size of a store and the storage space available.

Central executive according to the working-memory model, it is the controller of the system. It controls the flow of information and the processing; for example, it gets information into one stream, and controls whether the phonological loop or visuospatial scratchpad is needed.

Cognitive environment is the physical environment, emotional state and thinking state when encoding takes place and gives retrieval cues that activate a memory trace.

Computer analogy the idea that the brain can be likened to a computer, with input (from the senses), throughput (the processing) and output.

Conditions parts or aspects of the independent variable, such as whether words are in capitals (visual), whether they rhyme (auditory) or whether they fit into a sentence correctly (semantic).

Confabulation making up bits of an event when retelling it so that it makes more sense, which means a memory is not exactly like the perception of the event.

Confounding variables extraneous variables that seem to have affected the results of a study. For example, in a study memory was found to be better when recall was in the same context as learning; but in practice it was found that all those studied in the same context were younger than those studied in a different context, so age would be a confounding variable.

Context-dependent forgetting forgetting that occurs when the cues that were in the environment at encoding are missing at recall (leading to forgetting). There are cues about the situation and the context. This is as opposed to state-dependent forgetting.

Control group the group in an experiment that is producing a baseline measure of what would 'normally' happen without the manipulated condition in the experiment, such as learning a random list of letters rather than a grouped list and trying to recall them.

Counterbalancing alternating the conditions for each participant in an experiment to help to control for order effects in a repeated measures design. If there are two conditions, for example, the first participant does condition one followed by condition two. Then the second participant does condition two followed by condition one and so on.

Cue-dependent forgetting forgetting that occurs because of the lack of a retrieval cue in the cognitive environment at the time of retrieval so a memory trace is not activated.

Demand characteristics characteristics found when a participant's responses are affected by their guessing what the study is about.

Dependent variable (DV) what is being measured as a result of the experiment and as a result of the independent variable being manipulated. For example, when doing an experiment looking at the effect of interference on short-term memory in the number of letters recalled, the dependent variable of a study would be how many letters are recalled.

Directional hypothesis a hypothesis that predicts the direction of the results, such as whether more or fewer words are recalled. For example, 'recall of letters is greater if letters are grouped (chunked) than if they are not'.

Double-blind technique a procedure where neither the participants nor the person doing a study are aware of what is expected. It is used so that the experimenter cannot affect the results of the study because of their expectations.

Dual-task paradigm an experimental technique that involves two tasks, sometimes using the same systems and sometimes not to see what those systems are and how they work. For example, there can be two visual tasks, which the person will find hard, or a visual task and an auditory one, which they will find less hard. It was used by Baddeley and Hitch to test their working-memory model.

Duration the time something lasts. In the multi-store model it refers to how long a memory can stay in a store until it is lost (or the trace decays).

Ecological validity the extent to which the setting of a study is real life. If the setting is a natural one then the study has ecological validity and in that sense the findings are about real life. However, if the setting is not natural, as in a laboratory experiment, then the study lacks ecological validity, and the findings might not be about real life.

Encoding the first part of memory. Material has to be taken into the brain and held there somehow. Information comes from sense data and encoding can be visual, auditory or semantic — and perhaps in other forms such as touch. Encoding is about registering the information.

Engram the structural change in the brain that is a memory.

Experimental group the group in an experiment which is doing the condition that is of interest, such as learning grouped letters and then trying to recall them rather than a randomised list.

Experimenter effects features of the researcher that affect the results of a study, such as tone of voice or facial expression. These might lead the participant to react in certain ways.

Extraneous variables things that might affect the results of a study instead of or as well as the independent variable, such as noise, heat, light or some characteristic of the participants.

Fatigue effect an order effect that occurs when the first part or condition of a study is done better than a later one because the participant is tired by the time they do the second condition.

Field experiment an experiment with as many controls as possible and a manipulated independent variable, but conducted in the field rather than in a lab situation. In the field means in the participant's natural setting.

Forgetting not being able to recall something that could be recalled earlier. Forgetting is probably not one thing at all but a term for different ways of not remembering, including repression (which is motivated forgetting) and displacement (which is when new memories push old ones out).

Incidental learning learning that occurs when participants (or anyone) learn something without deliberately focusing on it, which would be intentional learning.

Independent variable (IV) what is being manipulated by the researcher. This is what is of interest in the study, and what is being tested. For example, when doing an experiment looking at the effect of interference on short-term memory in the number of letters recalled, the independent variable would be whether there is interference in the task or not.

Information processing the way that information comes into the brain via the senses, has something done to it (i.e. it is processed) and then there is an output in some form. There is a flow of information into, through, and out of the brain. This is what the cognitive approach is all about.

Intentional learning learning something by focusing on it and using strategies.

Intersection the crossing of searches in the spreading-activation model. A search from one starting node crosses with a search from another starting node.

Interval/ratio a level of measurement where data are real measurements such as time or temperature. A mean average is suitable.

Laboratory experiment an experiment in a controlled setting that is also artificial, i.e. not in the participant's natural environment. In a lab experiment there is often an experimental group and a control group, standardised instructions and good control over all variables other than the independent variable.

Levels of measurement ways in which data are scored or measured. There are three main levels of measurement for psychology at AS and A2: nominal, ordinal and interval/ratio.

Levels-of-processing framework the model of memory that says that the more semantic the processing, including elaboration and depth, the better the recall or recognition. Semantic means adding/using meaning while processing.

Lexical network the dictionary where words are kept (according to their sound, not their meaning), according to the spreading-activation model of memory.

Long-term memory the third store for memory, according to the multi-store model. Information that is rehearsed passes from the short-term memory to the long-term memory.

Mean a measure of central tendency (average) that is calculated by totalling the scores and then dividing by how many scores there are. It is only useful for data at the interval/ratio level of measurement.

Measures of central tendency averages, which include the mode, median and mean.

Measures of dispersion measures of how the data are spread around the mean. The range is a measure of dispersion, as is the standard deviation.

Median a measure of central tendency (average) that is worked out by finding the middle score. If there is no middle score the median is mid-way between the two either side of the middle. For example, out of ten scores the median is between the fifth and sixth score.

Memory encoding, storage and retrieval of experience. Without remembering, the person cannot function. There are different theories of memory, such as that it involves different levels of processing. Another theory suggests there is short-term and long-term memory.

Memory trace a piece of information laid down and retained as a result of the perception of an event.

Modality-specific when information is stored in the same form in which it is received. Information from the eyes is stored as an image, and from the ears is stored as sound.

Mode a measure of central tendency (average) that is worked out by finding the most common score. If there is more than one 'most common' score, then all are given. For example, if there are two modal scores, the data set is bi-modal.

Mode of representation the way memories are stored and the format they are stored in. A mode of representation or type of storage, could, for example, be visual or semantic.

Natural experiment an experiment that is usually in the field rather than in a lab because it involves finding a naturally occurring independent variable. For example, natural experiments have been done to look at the effects of television on children (such as aggression) when they can be measured before television is introduced in the area and then measured afterwards to see if there are effects. The researchers do not themselves make children have no television and then have television because that would not be ethical (or practical).

Node a concept or word that is part of the semantic network according to the spreading-activation model.

Nominal a level of measurement that means data are in categories only, with no numbers assigned. If data include whether someone is aggressive or not, that is nominal data. Measures of central tendency are not useful here.

Non-directional hypothesis a hypothesis in which no direction is predicted and the results can be either 'more' or 'less'. For example, 'recall of letters is affected by whether or not letters are grouped (chunked)'.

Null hypothesis the statement that any difference or relationship predicted in a study will be due to chance (in other words there is no relationship or difference as predicted). It is the hypothesis that is tested when using statistical tests.

Operationalise to make a variable measurable. If you wanted to test helpfulness it would be difficult to know where to start, but you could operationalise helpfulness by measuring whether someone asking for directions was shown the way or not.

Order effects effects that occur when the order of conditions in a study (in a repeated measures design) affects the responses of the participant. They include fatigue and practice effects.

Ordinal a level of measurement that means data are ranked so that the smallest score has rank 1 and so on. The mode and median are suitable averages to use.

Paired associate learning giving participants two words to learn as a pair and then testing them by giving them one of the words (usually the left-hand word in the pair) and asking for recall of the other word.

Parallel processing more than one operation or processing taking place in the brain at the same time.

Participant variables variables such as age, gender, experience and mood.

Phonological loop according to the working-memory model, it deals with sound information. There is an articulatory loop where rehearsal takes place too. The phonological loop has been called the 'inner ear' and the articulatory loop has been called the 'inner voice'. This helps to explain what they are for.

Practice effect an order effect that occurs when the second part or condition of a study is done better than the first because participants are practised by the time they do the second condition.

Primary memory refers to Type I processing, where information at one level is recycled at that level by repetition. For example, auditory information is 'heard' again. Type II processing involves adding something such as meaning.

Priming activating nodes and links ready for understanding and memory. For example, priming 'red' will activate relevant nodes such as other colours, fire, apple, cherries and roses.

Proactive interference the interference of something learned earlier with current learning. For example, learning Spanish first and French next means difficulty in learning the French.

Randomisation making the order in which the participant does the conditions random, to control for order effects in a repeated measures design. If a study has two conditions, for example, there can be a toss of the coin to see which condition the participant will do first.

Range a measure of dispersion. The range is calculated by taking the lowest score from the highest score. Sometimes you have to take 1 away from that calculation to get the range.

Rationalisation shortening a story to make it make sense. This shows that memory is reconstructive, as Bartlett claimed.

Replicability the extent to which a study is easy to repeat or replicate. A study is replicable if there are careful controls and if there is enough detail about the procedure to do the study again.

Retrieval getting to the memories stored in the brain. A problem with retrieval will lead to forgetting. One theory suggests that retrieval can be aided by cues.

Retrieval cue something in the person's cognitive environment at the time of retrieval that activates a memory trace.

Retroactive interference when something learned later gets in the way of something learned before. For example, learning Spanish first and French next means difficulty remembering the Spanish.

Schemata pre-existing ideas that have been built through experience and are plans for what we think will happen and what we know. For example, we might have a schema (the singular of schemata) for 'baking baked potatoes' or one for 'going on holiday on a train'. Our ideas affect how we remember events.

Semantic refers to the meaning of something. Semantic encoding would be registering the information in the form of its meaning, as you might with a word.

Semantic network part of the spreading-activation model of memory; it is the network of linked nodes, which contain concepts and ideas.

Sensory register the first store for memory, according to the multi-store model, where information comes into the brain from the senses. Information lasts less than a second and if it is attended to it goes to the short-term store. If it is not attended to it is then not available. Information is stored in the same form as it is received, so is modality-specific. Information from the eyes is stored as an image, and from the ears is stored as sound.

Serial processing performing one operation or process at a time.

Short-term memory the second store for memory, according to the multi-store model. Information that is attended to in the sensory register passes to the short-term memory; if it is then rehearsed it gets to the long-term memory.

Single blind technique used in a study to avoid expectations of participants affecting results and means the participants are not aware of which group they are in or what results are expected.

Situational variables variables to do with the situation, such as temperature, noise, interruptions and light.

Standard deviation a measure of dispersion that you can learn about for your course, but you do not have to. The standard deviation is worked out by taking all the scores away from the mean average to see how far the scores fluctuate around the mean. Whether they fluctuate or not can show how far they are spread around the mean average, which helps when interpreting the data.

Standardised instructions written sets of instructions to the participants in a study so that all participants get the same information and are not biased by being told something different.

State-dependent forgetting forgetting that occurs when the cues that were in the environment at encoding and are missing at recall (leading to forgetting) are cues about the state and mood of the individual. This is as opposed to context-dependent forgetting.

Storage the retention of information ready for retrieval. One type of forgetting is a problem with storage, another type can be a problem with retrieval.

Tachistoscope a box where the participant looks through a screen and can see letters, words, or whatever is of interest flash up for a very short time at the back of the box. The researcher can control the time the stimulus is exposed for and the time between exposures.

Theory an idea about why an event happens, usually based on previous theories and research.

Threshold firing in the brain does not have to be all or nothing (there is a signal or there is not) but there has to be a level of activity (or threshold) before a signal is triggered. Firing in the brain does not have to mean sending a signal, and not firing does not have to mean there isn't a signal. It is likely that there is a threshold of activity before which there is no signal and after which there is a firing of the signal. A set amount of activity is required rather than just 'off' or 'on'.

Variables whatever influences are likely to affect the experiment, including what is being tested, what is being measured, and anything else likely to affect the results. They include confounding variables, extraneous variables, the independent variable and the dependent variable. There are also situational variables and participant variables.

Visuospatial scratchpad according to the working-memory model, it deals with visual information. The scratchpad holds spatial information and information about images. The scratchpad could be called the 'inner eye'.

Unit 2

The psychodynamic approach

Anal character a character that develops when a child is fixated at the anal stage. The person can be anal-expulsive, which is messy, or anal-retentive, which is overly tidy. The anal-retentive character can be mean with money, obsessed with cleanliness and hoard possessions.

Anal-expulsive character a character that is messy and likely to enjoy messy pursuits.

Anal-retentive character a character that is mean, overly tidy, obsessed with cleanliness and likely to hoard.

Anal stage the second of Freud's psychosexual stages, from about 18 months to 2 years old. The focus of pleasure and sexual energy is the anus, and potty training is the key. The child might be messy when potty training or might hold back and either can lead to an 'anal' adult character.

Analysand the person undergoing the therapy of psychoanalysis.

Case history a research method used in case studies to describe the details of the study, and to give rich qualitative data.

Case study a research method gathering in-depth and detailed data about one individual or a small group. Triangulation is used to find themes from all the different data sources.

Castration fear how the boy thinks his father will punish him for having sexual feelings for his mother. It comes from his fear of his father and is resolved when the boy identifies with his father.

Conscious mind the part of the mind that contains the thoughts, feeling, ideas and other aspects of thinking that the individual knows about and can access easily.

Construct validity validity means data being about what they claim to be about (i.e. whether they represent reality). Construct validity relates specifically to the validity of what is being measured (whether that represents reality) rather than the setting or situation.

Correlation design a design in which one person generates two scores, both on a sliding scale. More than one participant is tested in this way and the two sets of scores are then tested to see if there is a relationship between them, such as one score rising as the other falls (this would be a negative correlation).

Credibility the extent to which the findings of research are believable. This is an important issue when doing scientific research.

Cross-sectional studies studies carried out in one moment of time, taking different participants at that time and comparing their performance in some way. A different way of carrying out a study is doing a longitudinal study.

Defence mechanisms strategies that help the ego to balance out the demands of the id and the superego. Some defence mechanisms push thoughts back into the unconscious and some turn them into something else to make them acceptable. Some defence mechanisms are repression, denial, projection, displacement and regression.

Denial a defence mechanism that explains how traumatic events seem to be ignored by the person experiencing them. It is as if they are in denial and refusing to accept what has happened. By keeping the memories unconscious they don't have to face them.

Displacement a defence mechanism whereby feelings that are dangerous to the person are transferred onto something safe.

Dream analysis listening to the manifest content of a dream (which is what is reported) and looking for the latent content (which is what the symbols in the manifest content are representing).

Ego the second part of the personality, which works on the reality principle. It is the rational part that works to satisfy the demands of the id and the superego.

Ego ideal part of the superego. It is what each person thinks they should be like.

Electra complex the process in which a girl has sexual feelings for the father and has penis envy, which she thinks her father can solve. She identifies with her mother to resolve her guilt at wanting her father. This occurs in the phallic stage.

Eros the life instinct, which is self-preservation and a sexual instinct; it is about biological arousal.

Fixation not resolving one of the stages of psychosexual development so that energy is needed to maintain the personality's balance.

Free association one of Freud's research methods, where the idea is for the patient to allow a stream of consciousness without stopping any thoughts. It was hoped that unconscious thoughts would be revealed, though in practice it was found difficult not to censor thoughts.

Hysteria the term for physical symptoms like blindness or being unable to move an arm when the symptoms have no physical cause. Freud suggested the cause was a mental one, stemming from the unconscious.

Id the first part of the personality, in the unconscious. It is the 'I want' part, which acts on the pleasure principle.

Identification the process by which a boy learns his gender behaviour, moral behaviour and conscience, through the Oedipus complex in the phallic stage.

Idiographic approach an approach to studying people that focuses on the individual and the detail rather than developing general laws about people.

Latent content the underlying meaning of a dream, which the analyst explains to the analysand by means of interpreting the symbols that are the manifest content.

Longitudinal studies studies that are done over time following the same participants, in order to compare their performance and thus draw conclusions about development in some way.

Manifest content the actual dream that a dreamer relates to the analyst, and the content of which is analysed by explaining it as being symbolic.

Negative correlation a relationship found when two scores from each participant are produced, and enough participants are tested; it shows that as one score rises the other falls. For example, as age rises speed of driving falls: a 60-year-old will drive more slowly than a 30-year-old.

Neuroses mental health problems in which the individual can have insight into their problems. They include such difficulties as phobias.

Nomothetic approach an approach to studying people that focuses on developing general laws about behaviour rather than on looking at individuals in detail.

Observation a research method used in psychology and usually means naturalistic observation. Observation is used in many different research methods, as most data are gathered by watching or listening and then recording, but in these cases observation is just one part of the research method in question. For example, Milgram watched and recorded participants' reactions in his study, but the study was a laboratory experiment. Naturalistic observations take place in a natural setting (as described in the context of the learning approach).

Oedipus complex the process in which a boy has sexual feelings for his mother, has castration fear because he thinks his father hates him as a rival for his mother, and resolves the problem by identifying with his father. This occurs in the phallic stage.

Oral character a character that develops when a child is fixated at the oral stage. Such people can be dependent, needy, obsessed with the mouth (e.g. smoking, pen sucking) and sarcastic.

Oral stage the first of Freud's psychosexual stages, from birth to around 18 months old. The focus of pleasure and sexual energy is the mouth and nursing and sucking are the key. The child might not get the right amount of oral stimulation and then as an adult might have an oral character.

Penis envy what the girl feels because she learns she does not have a penis and neither does her mother. So she turns to her father, thinking he can give her a penis. This is part of the Electra complex in the phallic stage.

Phallic character self-assured, reckless, vain and proud. There might also be problems because of inappropriate gender behaviour at the phallic stage.

Phallic stage the third of Freud's psychosexual stages. In this stage the Oedipus complex occurs, which is where the boy has sexual feelings for his mother, has castration fear because he thinks his father hates him as a rival for his mother, and resolves the problem by identifying with his father. This identification gives the superego and gender behaviour as the boy takes on his father's beliefs and behaviour.

Positive correlation a relationship found when two scores from each participant are produced, and enough participants are tested; it shows that as one score rises the other rises too. For example, as age rises, the time taken to react to a stimulus rises. A 60-year-old will take longer to react than a 30-year-old, for example.

Preconscious mind the part of the mind that contains thoughts and ideas that the individual can access although they are not currently conscious.

Projection a defence mechanism whereby one person's feelings are said to be the feelings of another person.

Psychoses mental health problems in which the individual cannot have insight into their problems because of the nature of the difficulties. They include such problems as schizophrenia.

Regression a defence mechanism whereby the individual goes back to a childlike state to avoid unacceptable impulses.

Repression a defence mechanism whereby information is forgotten, or rather not remembered, because it is traumatic and would threaten the individual in some way.

Scattergraph a graph used for correlation data where each point on the graph represents one person's score on two scales. This is the only time a scattergraph should be used to represent data. A line of best fit can show if there is a correlation or not, prior to carrying out a statistical test.

Self-report data data where the participant's answers report on their own feelings or circumstances, such as whether they are quiet by nature, or generous.

Slip of the tongue saying one thing and meaning another, such as talking about 'erection' when meaning 'rejection', or 'orgasm' when meaning 'organism'. The mistake or slip that is made reveals repressed thoughts.

Superego the third part of the personality, which works on the morality principle. It is made up of the conscience, which is given by parents and society, and the ego ideal, which is the person the individual thinks they should be.

Symbol analysis translating the manifest content of a dream, which represents the latent content. The manifest content is symbolic and can be interpreted to reveal unconscious desires.

Thanatos the death instinct, which is the ultimate way to reduce the arousal of the life instinct.

Transference the term Freud used when a patient transferred feelings onto the analyst. The feelings can be love or hate and transference is an important part of the cure.

Triangulation gathering data by different means about one person or event. The researcher then pools the findings to develop themes when analysing.

Unconscious mind the unconscious part of the mind that according to Freud is hidden so that we cannot access it. It holds thoughts and feelings that, although not accessible, have a strong effect on our behaviour and our lives. Sometimes that effect is negative, but if such unconscious thoughts are made conscious, their negative effect is removed.

The biological approach

Ablation a research method used to study the brain, to find out which part carries out which function. Ablation means a part is removed (if a part is just damaged, that is lesioning).

Adoption studies studies where children who are adopted are looked at, mainly because their environment will not be the same as for their biological family and yet they will share their genes with their biological family. So it can be seen if a characteristic is attributable to nature or nurture.

Androgenital syndrome a genetic disorder that is caused by a deficiency in the hormones aldosterone and cortisol and an overproduction of androgens.

Central nervous system the brain and spinal cord. The brain is within the skull and the spinal cord is set within the vertebrae. In the embryo a tube separates into the brain and the spinal cord and then there are further subdivisions. The brain itself is split into different parts.

Chromosome a double chain of DNA; there are 23 pairs of chromosomes in the human organism.

Concordance rate the extent to which pairs of twins share a characteristic.

Critical values tables tables of figures against which the results of a statistical test are checked for significance. There are special tables for each test.

Degrees of freedom (df) the number of cells in a table that are free to vary if the column and the row totals are known.

Dizygotic (DZ) twins non-identical twins from two eggs, who share 50% of their genes like any brother or sister.

DNA a twisted thread made up of 23 chromosome pairs (in humans) divided into genes. DNA is made up of a coded sequence of four chemical bases. The coded sequence is what makes someone unique because there are so many combinations of those four chemical bases.

Dominant gene a gene that always gives its characteristic because it needs to be on only one of a pair of chromosomes.

Epigenetic modification the term for how different environmental influences on an individual over time affect which genes are switched on and off.

Gender the term used instead of 'sex' when referring to males and females with regard to their development and behaviour in more than a biological way.

Genes the sections of DNA that make people who they are. A gene consists of a long strand of DNA, and genes are set up in such a way that they are a blueprint for what people are like.

Genome the term for all the genes in the cell of an organism.

Genotype the instruction from our genes to make us what we are.

Hermaphrodite an organism that has characteristics of both males and females.

Holistic approach the idea that to find out about something, the whole must be studied, not the parts. For example, you can study a person's levels of aggression by scanning and seeing activity in the limbic system, but real-life aggression is more complex: it has a trigger, a type (physical or verbal, for example) and a background. The opposite of a holistic approach could be said to be a reductionist approach.

Hormones chemical messengers that work more slowly than neurotransmitters and are carried in the blood stream. They are produced by the endocrine system; glands in that system include the pineal gland, pituitary gland and thyroid.

Inferential statistics tests to see whether variables being studied are different or related enough to draw conclusions to that effect. Tests include the Spearman, Mann Whitney U, and Chi-squared.

Lateralisation how far one half of the brain is used rather than the other. Males are said to be more lateralised than females, because males use the right side of the brain more than the left, whereas females use both sides more equally.

Lesioning a research method used to study the brain and what part is for what purpose. It involves damaging parts of the brain, as opposed to ablation, which means a part is actually removed. Research using lesioning is mostly done on animals or as part of a medical procedure on humans, not just for research purposes.

Level of significance the level of probability that results are due to chance; the researcher will choose a level to say that at this level or lower the hypothesis will be accepted as statistically significant. For example, a researcher might accept that 1 in 20 or fewer results will be due to chance ($p \leq 0.05$) and then claim that the hypothesis was 'true'. This is normal practice in psychology, though a 1 in 100 level ($p \leq 0.01$) is better.

Monozygotic (MZ) twins identical twins from one egg, who share 100% of their genes.

Myelination a covering (myelin sheath) around the nerve fibre for protection.

N the number of scores in a list, which will be the number of participants.

Nature–nurture debate the question of how far a characteristic comes from our nature (what we are born with, which is down to our genes) and how far it comes from our nurture (what we experience from our environment as we develop, which is down to our upbringing).

Neurotransmitters chemicals in the brain that act as messengers and either cross from one neurone to the receptors of another neurone over the synaptic gap or do not fit the receptors so are blocked.

Observed value the result of a statistical test once carried out. For Spearman the test result is called ρ (rho). For the Mann Whitney U the test result is called U. For the Chi-squared test the test result is called Chi-squared and is written χ^2. Really the observed value is the term used for the Chi-squared test more than for the others, which are just called ρ and U respectively.

One- or two-tailed test a test carried out depending on whether the hypothesis being tested is directional or non-directional. A directional hypothesis requires a one-tailed test and a non-directional hypothesis requires a two-tailed test.

Phenotype what we are, arising from the interaction of our genes with our environment.

Pro-speciesism the attitude that it is the duty of humans to improve their own quality of life by whatever means, even using animals, so it is ethically acceptable to use animals.

Receptors places on neurones on one side of the synaptic cleft. Neurotransmitters that are waiting on the other side either fit into the receptors and so cross the gap, or do not fit and so are released into the gap, which means that uptake is blocked.

Recessive gene a gene that needs more than one copy for its characteristic to be produced, so that that characteristic may not appear in an organism even though a gene for it is present. In a later generation, if two copies of the recessive gene are inherited, that characteristic may appear.

Reductionist approach a search for facts that looks at parts in order to draw conclusions rather than studying the whole (which would be a holistic approach). For example, looking at which parts of the brain are activated when someone is talking is a reductionist approach because it looks only at brain activity, whereas taking account of what is being said and why, as well as how other decisions are made and who is speaking, would be a holistic approach.

Reproductive hormones hormones that link to sex differentiation. They include oestrogen for women and testosterone for men.

Sex the term used for biological differences between males and females, as opposed to the term 'gender', which is usually used when environmental aspects are also included.

Synapse the gap between the dendrites of one neurone and the axon terminal of another neurone. Whether or not the neurotransmitter produced passes across the gap to the receptors waiting for it decides whether a message passes on or is blocked.

Twin studies comparisons of MZ and DZ twins on certain characteristics to see if there are differences between how frequently the MZ twins and how frequently the DZ twins share the characteristic. If there are quite strong differences then that characteristic is said to have a genetic basis, at least to an extent.

The learning approach

Access getting permission to carry out a study. Access can be a problem for ethical or practical reasons.

Aversion therapy a therapy based on classical conditioning principles. An inappropriate pleasure response, such as liking alcohol, is replaced with an aversion to the stimulus, for example by pairing alcohol with an emetic drug that makes a person feel sick. Finally they feel sick in response to alcohol so they stop drinking.

Conditioned response (CR) in classical conditioning, the reflex or involuntary response that has been conditioned to occur to a specific stimulus that would not usually elicit that response. The specific stimulus (the conditioned stimulus) has to be paired with an unconditioned stimulus to get the required response, and only when that conditioned stimulus on its own gets the response is the response called a conditioned response. In Pavlov's experiments one conditioned response is salivation to a bell.

Conditioned stimulus (CS) in classical conditioning, the specific stimulus that is deliberately paired with an unconditioned stimulus so that eventually the conditioned stimulus alone gets the response, which is then called a conditioned response. In Pavlov's experiments one conditioned stimulus is a bell.

Covert with the observation being done secretly so that the participants do not know that it is taking place.

Ecological validity the extent to which the setting of a study is real life, so that data are real and the study is (with regard to the setting at least) gathering the data it is claiming to gather.

Extinction in classical conditioning, when a previously conditioned response to a conditioned stimulus no longer occurs because the pairing of the unconditioned stimulus with the conditioned stimulus to get the association no longer occurs.

Graduated exposure therapy another name for systematic desensitisation.

Imitation one of the processes of observational learning, in social learning theory. Once behaviour has been modelled, it is imitated, depending on certain circumstances such as the observed consequences of the behaviour for the model.

Inter-observer reliability agreement between observers. When more than one observer is used in one study, their observations can be compared. If their observations agree, it can be said that there is inter-observer reliability, because in a way the study was done twice and the results compared.

Introspection thinking about one's own thinking. A participant can think about their own thoughts and how they process information and explain those processes to a researcher.

Involuntary response the reflex that happens after a stimulus has occurred. It is not under someone's control and is bound to happen, unlike a voluntary response.

Law of effect Thorndike's explanation of operant conditioning. He says that if the effect of behaviour is rewarding, then that behaviour will be repeated.

Naturalistic observation a research method in which the setting is a natural one for the participants and data are gathered only by observation.

Non-participant observations studies in which the observer is not part of the situation and is an outsider looking in.

Observational learning learning that takes place by observing a role model and imitating their behaviour. It depends on certain factors, such as whether the model is rewarded for that behaviour.

Overt with participants knowing that the observation is taking place and being aware of all aspects of the study.

Participant observations studies in which the observer is part of the situation being observed, either because they 'infiltrate' or because they already are a member of the group or part of the situation.

Phobia a fear that is so strong that it affects someone's life and stops them doing things. A fear is not as strong as a phobia; a phobia is a mental illness — a neurosis that can be treated by classical conditioning principles and other therapies.

Primary data data that researchers gather themselves rather than using data already gathered, which are secondary data.

Primary reinforcement a reward that satisfies a basic need such as hunger, thirst, warmth or shelter. For rats food pellets are primary reinforcements, for example. For humans money is a secondary reinforcement.

Response something that happens after a stimulus is received, such as blinking the eye when a puff of air is blown onto it. This is an involuntary response, which means it is bound to happen and is not controlled.

Response cost part of a token economy programme. Tokens or points can be taken away for undesired behaviour as a form of punishment.

Role model someone whose behaviour is observed and then in certain circumstances is imitated. A role model tends to have some importance for the observer. For children, parents, peers, media personalities and other significant others are likely to be role models.

Secondary data data that are already gathered for some other purpose or by some other researcher.

Secondary reinforcement a reward that does not itself satisfy a basic need but can be used to satisfy one. For example, money is a secondary reinforcement for humans because it buys what they need.

Shaping gradually reinforcing small actions by rewarding them; then withholding the reward until the behaviour is a bit closer to what is required; and proceeding in that way until the actual required behaviour is exhibited and can be rewarded.

Social learning theory (SLT) the theory that people learn by observing others. This is observational learning — people can watch what others do and copy their actions, thus learning new behaviours.

Spontaneous recovery in classical conditioning, the spontaneous reappearance of a conditioned response after it has been extinguished. A conditioned response can be extinguished because the unconditioned stimulus is no longer paired with the conditioned stimulus, but it can then sometimes reappear of its own accord.

Stimulus something in the environment that produces a response (which occurs because of the stimulus). For example, the stimulus of blowing on the eyes gives a response of a blink.

Structured observation a study in which data are collected by observing and there is no manipulation of the independent variable, but the situation is structured (set up).

Tallying making a mark against the behaviours observed when carrying out an observation. Tallying gives quantitative data.

Time-sampling making a tally mark in an observation every minute or at some other specified time slot. This means a better picture is given of what happens during the observation than recording only changes of activity, for example, because the time during which one activity is carried out is recorded.

Token economy programme a therapy based on operant conditioning principles, where a desired behaviour (for example, in a prison or mental health institution) is rewarded with a token and the tokens can be exchanged for desired goods.

Trial and error learning learning that occurs at first by accident; then the reward is reached; and then the behaviour is repeated to get the reward.

Unconditioned response (UCR) in classical conditioning, the response that is automatically given to an unconditioned stimulus. For example, an eye blink is the unconditioned response to a puff of air on the eye, which is the unconditioned stimulus. In one of Pavlov's experiments the unconditioned response is salivation (to food).

Unconditioned stimulus (UCS) in classical conditioning, the stimulus that automatically gets a response that is involuntary and a reflex. An example is a puff of air on the eye, which is an unconditioned stimulus because it gives rise automatically to an eye blink, which is the unconditioned response. In one of Pavlov's experiments the unconditioned stimulus is food.

Vicarious reinforcement the part of social learning theory that emphasises how imitation depends on the consequences of behaviour — whether the model is reinforced or punished for their behaviour.

Voluntary response something that someone chooses to do after a stimulus or before a reward or punishment. This is as opposed to an involuntary response, such as blinking, which is not under the person's control and is a reflex.

Questions
&
Answers

- Questions are presented in three sections, one for each of the three approaches.
- Remember the paper will not split the questions up by approach, so expect any of the approaches for any question. Expect the paper to ask about any of the six areas within each approach at any time.
- To remind you, the three approaches are the psychodynamic approach, the biological approach and the learning approach. The six areas are the definitions, methodology, content, studies in detail, key issue and practical.
- Choose one approach and revise the material using this unit guide. Work through the questions for your chosen approach, answering them yourself without reading the advice on how to answer the question and without reading the answer given.
- Then mark your own answers, and read through the advice on what is required. Did you interpret the question successfully? Read through the answers given and note where the marks were awarded. Finally, read through the examiner's comments to see what a full answer should include.
- Once you have prepared answers for all the questions in a particular approach, answer them again but this time choose a different topic. For example, if you described a theory of learning within the learning approach, describe another theory of learning. If the question is about one in-depth area (e.g. genes in the biological approach), answer it as if it were about the other in-depth area (e.g. hormones). In this way you are making up your own questions, which is useful preparation for the examination.
- When you think you have revised enough, there is a paper that you can work through, with a mark scheme, in the sample assessment materials prepared for your course. You can find that paper on the Edexcel website (www.edexcel.org.uk).

Examiner's comments

All questions and answers are followed by examiner's comments. These are preceded by the icon *e*. They indicate where credit is due and point out areas for improvement, specific problems and common errors such as poor time management, lack of clarity, weak or non-existent development, irrelevance, misinterpretation of the question and mistaken meanings of terms.

Section 1

The psychodynamic approach

Definitions

(1) Consider the terms below and match them to the definitions given. There are some definitions that do not fit. Write the term on the correct line in each case.

(6 marks, AO1)

Terms: id, ego, superego, anal stage, phallic stage, defence mechanism

Definitions/statements	Write in the correct term (6 terms)
Where the conscience is	
Works on the pleasure principle	
Is the third psychosexual stage	
Focuses on genes	
Repression	
Focuses on potty training	
Involves modelling and imitation	
Works on the reality principle	

The six terms relate to the psychodynamic approach. Match them to the definitions/statements. Six of the definitions fit, two do not. This question could be set up differently as a multiple-choice question.

Answer

Definitions/statements	Write in the correct term (6 terms)
Where the conscience is	superego
Works on the pleasure principle	id
Is the third psychosexual stage	phallic stage
Focuses on genes	
Repression	defence mechanism
Focuses on potty training	anal stage
Involves modelling and imitation	
Works on the reality principle	ego

These are all correct. This sort of question should not be difficult. Make sure you know what all the terms mean.

(2) **What does it mean to say that the psychodynamic approach is about the influence of unconscious processes? Explain this and give one example as an illustration.**

(3 marks, AO1)

 You need to explain what 'unconscious processes' means with reference to Freud's ideas, and in your answer give an example of one or more unconscious processes. Assume 1 mark for the example, 1 mark for a brief explanation and 1 further mark if the explanation is thorough.

Answer

Unconscious processes according to Freud consist of thoughts and wishes in the mind that are not accessible and make up much of the mind. They affect a person's behaviour and thoughts even though the thoughts are not known consciously. ✔✔ An example is when something traumatic has happened to someone but they have no conscious knowledge of it. ✔

 This answer gets all 3 marks. The first two sentences give a rich enough explanation to get 2 marks although more could be added, such as the idea that there is a conscious, a preconscious and an unconscious and the unconscious is by far the largest area, or that the id part of the personality is unconscious.

(3) **The psychodynamic approach has been criticised as not being scientific. Science focuses on objective and measurable data. Explain why the psychodynamic approach might be said to be unscientific.** (4 marks, AO3/AO2)

 This question is not likely to be part of the 'definitions' area of the approach but could be part of the methodology section. It is here, however, to show you that the sections are not separate in the exam and you can use information from more than one section when answering a question. This question is likely to be seen as being about methodology and therefore AO3, but could be evaluation of the approach and therefore AO2.

Answer

The psychodynamic approach involves concepts such as the unconscious and the id, the part of the personality found in the unconscious. The unconscious is not something that can be measured as it is a concept not part of the brain so the approach is said to be unscientific. ✔ Specific measurable data cannot be gathered. The id too, and other parts of the personality, are not measurable, although concepts within other personality theories (such as introversion) are not measurable either. ✔ Also Freud had to interpret the data he gathered because what is in the unconscious has to be uncovered in ways such as interpreting symbols. ✔ Science needs to be objective because subjective data might not be repeatable or testable. Interpretation is perhaps personal and subjective, so again it is said that the approach is not scientific. ✔

📝 There is easily enough here for the 4 marks. The two areas (measurable and objective) are both addressed. There are other features of science that could be addressed, such as reliability, but this answer is enough for the marks. There are no marks for description, but it is necessary to give some description (such as about the unconscious and the id) to explain the point (e.g. about the concepts not being measurable).

■ ■ ■

Methodology

(1) Explain two problems with using qualitative data in psychological research.

(4 marks, AO3)

📝 Your course requires you to know about reliability, validity, subjectivity, objectivity and generalisability with regard to qualitative data. Use two of these as the two problems and expand on what you mean when you explain the problem. This will give you the 2 marks for each problem: 1 mark is likely to be for identifying the problem and 1 for explaining it more fully.

Answer 1

Qualitative data means giving numbers such as percentages, and this is useful as analysis is easy. Also qualitative data are found in structured interviews, such as asking for 'yes' and 'no' answers.

Answer 2

Qualitative data are hard to generalise from ✔ because they involve detailed evidence from one unique individual. Data from other individuals, even if they are similar in some way, are likely to be different. This means each set of data is not likely to apply to anyone else and is unique. ✔ Qualitative data are also unlikely to be reliable ✔ for similar reasons. It will be hard to repeat the study because on a different occasion or with a different researcher the data might be different so not reliable. ✔

📝 Answer 1 gets 0 marks because it is about quantitative data. Make sure you read the question carefully.

📝 Answer 2 gets all 4 marks. There are 2 marks for the two problems — lack of generalisability and lack of reliability. Both issues are explained clearly so the 2 other marks are given as well.

(2) Describe and evaluate the case study as a research method used in the psycho-dynamic approach.   (12 marks, AO3)

> This is an essay question so would be marked using levels/banding, not point by point. There would be marks for how the essay is written, including spelling, grammar, structure and use of terms. There would also be marks for the description. Then you can assume that you would only get over about 6 marks if you address the evaluation part of the question as well. Remember to focus only on Freud's style of case study, though some general points apply to both Freud's case studies and general case studies, so they would be credited too. Any example you use should be from the psychodynamic approach. An example of a study is a good idea for 1 mark but needs explaining rather than just mentioning.

Answer

Freud used case studies to develop his psychodynamic theory that a child grows through psychosexual stages and that there are three parts to the personality. He used psychoanalysis to listen to what one unique individual was saying and then analysed the information by interpreting symbols and feeding back to the person to explain their behaviour or problems. He gathered a great deal of in-depth information from one individual, which makes his research method a case study. One example is Little Hans, a young child whose parents wrote letters to Freud giving information about Little Hans's phobia of horses, among a lot of other detail. A problem with the case study method is that qualitative data are gathered and they are not generalisable (true of other people), because only one unique individual is studied so the data are only relevant to that one person. Also case studies tend not to give reliable data because they are hard to repeat. Freud's study of Little Hans could not be repeated because he would have gone through his crisis with Freud's help so the same data would not be available. Even if someone re-analysed the story, it was written up by Freud so data would have been selected and interpreted. This means case study evidence is not objective either.

> This answer both describes and evaluates case studies in the approach as a research method, so the marks can go into 6+. The description is reasonably detailed, with a clear example and comments about how the case study is carried out. The evaluation considers generalisability, reliability and objectivity, all of which are made relevant. It is clear that all three terms are understood. This answer can be linked back to the earlier questions on whether the psychodynamic approach is scientific and the two problems with qualitative data; the same material can be used for these different questions. Evaluation could have included whether the data are valid or not. There is a lot of relevant information though more detail could have been given, so this is a good answer that would get around 9 or 10 of the 12 marks. Terms are used correctly and the essay is well organised, with evaluation given after description, so the 'communication' element of the essay is fine.

(3) What is meant by the two terms 'cross-sectional' and 'longitudinal' when it comes to research methods in psychology? (4 marks, AO3)

🖉 This question gives 2 marks each to two definitions.

Answer

Cross-sectional studies are those where the data are gathered at one moment in time with participants in two different groups, so they use an independent groups design. The same tests or tasks are carried out on the two groups and are then compared. ✔✔ Longitudinal studies are those where data are gathered over a period of time using the same participants each time. The same tests or tasks are carried out with the same people over a period of time, which can be months or years. ✔✔

🖉 All 4 marks are gained because it is clear that both terms are clearly understood. An example could add to the explanation but is not needed here, though it is useful to add an example to make sure you show clear understanding. The marks are shown as double marks because you do not need to make two separate points for each: a detailed and clear explanation gets 2 marks.

■ ■ ■

Content

(1) Outline two defence mechanisms. (4 marks, AO1)

🖉 This is a straightforward definitions question asking for two defence mechanisms. You will have studied repression and one other, and as this book uses denial that is the one used here. Often there is 1 mark for identifying the two defence mechanisms in a question like this, then there are 3 other 'outline' marks. One way of making sure you get the marks is to use examples.

Answer

Repression means that information is forgotten because it is in the unconscious ✔ and denial ✔*(identification mark)* means that something is not acknowledged.

🖉 Two defence mechanisms are given so there is 1 mark for identifying them. Then there is 1 mark for saying that forgetting is having information in the unconscious, though some more about motivated forgetting or an example would be needed for another mark. Saying that denial is not acknowledging something is just saying the same thing in a different way so there is no other mark. Explaining more about denial and giving an example would get the other marks.

(2) Describe how Freud explained that a boy learns appropriate gender behaviour.

(6 marks, AO1)

🖉 You need to give a lot of detail about Freud's ideas about gender development. All the marks are for description. You could give one example, which is likely to get 1 mark.

Answer

Freud thought that boys develop their gender behaviour in the phallic stage, the third psychosexual stage. ✔ He explained that boys go through the Oedipus complex, which is resolved when a boy identifies with his father and takes on his father's (male) behaviour. ✔ In the phallic stage sexual energy is focused on the genitals and the boy has unconscious feelings for his mother. ✔ But he has castration fear as well, fearing his father as a rival for his mother's affections. ✔ The fear and anxiety need to be resolved by the ego, so to do this the boy identifies with (becomes) his father and takes on his gender behaviour. ✔ Little Hans was an example that Freud used, as Little Hans wanted his father to go away and seemed to want to be with his mother. When Little Hans used role play with dolls and said that he (Hans) was the father, Hans's mother was the mother and Hans's father was the grandfather, then Freud thought that Hans had resolved the Oedipus complex and had passed through the stage. ✔

🖉 1 mark is for stating which stage is involved (the third stage) and adding a bit more. 1 mark is for starting an explanation of the Oedipus complex and 1 mark is for explaining the importance of the genitals and feelings for the mother. A fourth mark is for mentioning castration fear and the fifth mark is for explaining how the anxiety is overcome and how this links to gender behaviour. 1 mark is given for the example of Little Hans, which is well explained at the end; expect only 1 mark for examples. All 6 marks are gained.

■ ■ ■

Studies in detail

(1) Outline the findings (results and/or conclusions) of two studies in the psycho-dynamic approach.

(6 marks, AO1)

🖉 Assume there are 3 marks for each study and give the results and the conclusions or just one of these elements for each. You will have studied Little Hans and one other, which in this book is Axline's study of Dibs, so that is used in this answer.

Answer

The Little Hans study showed that Little Hans's phobia of horses was really a fear of his father and the horses were a symbol for the father. ✔ The dark round the eyes represented glasses, for example. When Freud explained this symbolism to

Hans's father and the father explained to Little Hans, this was accepted as an explanation and Freud took it as evidence for the Oedipus complex. ✔ In the Oedipus complex, according to Freud, a boy will fear his father because of having sexual focus on his mother. ✔ The Dibs case study showed that Dibs was able to use play therapy to demonstrate problems he was having, ✔ and this play therapy seemed to be cathartic in the sense that by acting out his feelings Dibs was able to overcome them. ✔

📝 This answer gets 5 of the 6 marks. More needs to be said about the Dibs case study, perhaps an example of how the 'Papa' soldier was buried or how Dibs feared being locked up, and an explanation of what this 'meant'.

(2) Evaluate the Little Hans study. (6 marks, AO2)

📝 This is a straightforward question. You need to make enough points to get the 6 marks. This means either 6 separate clear points or some points elaborated enough to get more than 1 mark for them. You can evaluate the study itself, or the case study method, or the approach itself, as long as you make the points relevant to the study.

Answer

- A case study so not generalisable.
- A case study so not reliable because hard to replicate as the study would change the situation. ✔
- The concepts are not measurable.
- The study is not scientific because Freud had to interpret the data and also Little Hans did not give the information directly, so his parents also interpreted and selected it. ✔

📝 Avoid using bullet points in any psychology answer. A bullet point is likely to be too short to make the point properly and this is what has happened in this answer. Two of the bullet points get a mark each because the points are clearly made. However, the other two bullet points do not get marks because, although you can see what the answer is trying to say, the points do not show understanding of the issues. If these two points had been made properly they would have gained marks, and some more elaboration on the other points could have gained more marks as well. This answer gets 2 of the 6 marks.

■ ■ ■

Key issue

(1) Use the following three concepts from the psychodynamic approach to explain a key issue: unconscious, repression, one or more features of the personality.

(4 marks, AO2)

This is a different way of asking a key issues question. It requires you to use your prepared key issue, which in this book is the issue of false memory, and explain it using the three concepts. This means explaining the key issue and making sure you bring in all three concepts. This should not be hard as these three concepts are central to the approach.

Answer

It has been claimed that what is uncovered during psychoanalysis could be false memories rather than genuinely repressed memories. If they are repressed memories then these would be hidden in the unconscious by symbols and the analysis could uncover the memories by interpreting the symbols. ✔ Repression is a defence mechanism to protect the individual so it would be expected that the memories are traumatic. The memories would be hidden in the unconscious that is not accessible to the individual so has to be uncovered by means such as interpreting symbols. ✔ The id part of the personality is in the unconscious and is about wishes and desires that are not in some way allowed, so repressed traumatic memories may involve such desires, which the ego has buried. ✔ However, it is possible that the power of the analyst has led the person to accept their interpretation (that the memories are real and were repressed) when in fact the memories are false memories and not true at all. ✔

This answer gets the 4 marks for explaining the issue well using the concepts of repression, the unconscious and the id part of the personality. The answer is clearly focused and uses terms well.

■ ■ ■

Practical

For the psychodynamic approach you will have carried out a correlational study. Answer the following questions with your practical in mind.

(1) (a) Give the aim of your study. (1 mark, AO3)

Just state the aim — the purpose of your study. The marks will be in bands rather than ticks, but ticks are given here to explain what would gain marks.

Answer

The aim was to see if type of parenting affects how tidy someone is. ✔

This is fine — it can be brief for the 1 mark available.

(b) Give one example of a rating scale you used. (2 marks, AO3)

You will have used a rating scale to gather at least some of your data. Say what you did. There are 2 marks because if the answer is thorough it can deserve 2 marks, rather than 1 for a brief answer (this is how levels marking works, rather than point by point).

Answer

A Likert-type scale was used and I asked the participant to rate their tidiness using the statement 'I am a tidy person' I gave them the options of strongly agree (5 marks), agree (4 marks), not sure (3 marks), disagree (2 marks), strongly disagree (1 mark). ✔✔

🖉 This gets the 2 marks as it is thorough and clear. 1 mark would be for a briefer answer (and 0 marks if not relevant at all).

(c) Explain what is meant by self-report data using an example from your study.

(2 marks, AO3)

🖉 This question asks for a definition and an example so assume 1 mark for each — though marking would be using levels.

Answer

Self-report data means getting the information from someone who talks about themselves and their own experiences, feelings and so on. They report on themselves. In my study I asked participants to rate themselves on their tidiness and their upbringing so both these scales involve self-report data. ✔✔

🖉 This answer easily gets the 2 marks because the definition is clear and the example is clear as well.

(d) Explain how you addressed one ethical issue.

(2 marks, AO3)

🖉 There are 2 marks so you need to explain the issue and how you dealt with it. A brief answer will get 1 mark, a more thorough one 2 marks.

Answer

I made sure data were confidential because I did not ask for names and I just used numbers to relate the two questionnaires to one another for analysis. I did not know the participants myself — or at least did not know which data went with which person — so the data were bound to be confidential. I also did not let anyone else know who the participants were. ✔✔

🖉 Two marks are gained easily as the ethical issue is clearly understood and explained by showing how it was dealt with in the study.

(e) What is meant by the term 'apparatus'? Outline your apparatus.

(3 marks, AO3)

🖉 You need to explain what apparatus is and then say what your apparatus was. This question is marked using levels, but assume 1 mark for the definition and 2 marks for your own apparatus.

Answer

Apparatus in a study is what is used to gather the data and includes everything from pencil and paper to a list of words or questionnaire. ✔ In my study I used two questionnaires on an A4 sheet of paper, one on each side. I needed some pens as well but nothing else, as there was nothing to time, for example. ✔✔

This is fine for the 3 marks because it is clear that the candidate knows what apparatus is. Their own apparatus is quite simple but for this study that is all they needed. The answer shows this simplicity by adding a bit about what was not needed, which is a good idea to make sure you say enough for this sort of question. In a memory experiment, for example, you may have had more to say.

Section 2

The biological approach

Definitions

(1) List four terms that are used when describing how neurotransmitters work in the brain and for each briefly explain their part in the process. (8 marks, AO1)

> 🖉 There are 2 marks for each term and brief explanation of what it means. Use the key terms for this approach (though you could use other aspects of neurotransmitter functioning and you would get credit, as the question does not ask for the key terms).

Answer

The synapse ✔ is the gap between the terminal buttons of one neurone and the dendrites of another neurone. ✔ The receptors ✔ are at the dendrites and receive the neurotransmitter if there is a fit and if they are not already 'filled'. ✔ The neurone ✔ is the term for the cell body, axon, terminal buttons and dendrites — it is the whole section that takes up the neurotransmitter, ✔ which releases an electrical impulse ✔down the axon, which releases neurotransmitter and the process continues. ✔ So impulse is another term.

> 🖉 This answer gets all 8 marks. The four terms are synapse, receptors, neurone and impulse, though in fact the axon, dendrites and the cell body are also mentioned and could get credit. All four terms are identified and it is clear what part they play in the process, so each gets the 2 marks.

(2) What is meant by the biological approach? (3 marks, AO1)

> 🖉 This question asks you to define the approach. You can describe one main feature of the approach in depth or more than one in some breadth. Either would be appropriate.

Answer

The biological approach focuses on the nature of a person including their genetic inheritance. Genes are the blueprint for what the person will be like and they trigger proteins according to pre-programmed sequences. ✔ These sequences, for example, dictate whether a fetus is male or female by triggering certain hormones; for example, androgens trigger male genitalia to develop alongside a hormone that prevents female development. ✔ The biological approach also considers other aspects of nature, such as focusing on how the brain works using neurotransmitter functioning. ✔

This answer gets the 3 marks and the detail about genes is in fact probably worth all 3 marks in itself. As the answer gives some detail about neurotransmitters as well, that point gets the final mark in this case.

■ ■ ■

Methodology

(1) Give one example of how a control group could be used in a study, and when giving your example make sure you show what a control group is for. The study can be a real one or one you have designed yourself. (3 marks, AO3)

As the example of the use of a control group can be made up, you could give one of your own. Alternatively you could give a real example, such as Raine et al. (1997). There are 3 marks so there might be 1 mark for identifying a suitable example and then 2 further marks for explaining the purpose of the control group.

Answer

Raine et al. (1997) used a control group in their study. The experimental group was a group of 41 people charged with murder or manslaughter and they were tested using PET scanning to look at their brain structure and functioning. A control group of non-murderers was tested as well so that the brain structure and functioning of the experimental group had a baseline measure (a 'normal' group) to compare it ✔ with. The control group was matched with the experimental group in many ways — age, gender, mental health, for example. ✔ They had to be as near as possible to the experimental group so that the only difference was whether the person had been charged with murder or manslaughter or not. Otherwise other differences might have caused any brain differences. ✔

This is a thorough answer. Another mark if there were one available could have been given for the penultimate sentence where the 'only difference' comment is made.

(2) Evaluate twin studies as a research method. (4 marks, AO3)

You do not have to describe twin studies here, just say what is good or bad about them. There are 4 marks, so making four points is the straightforward way to get the marks, although if you elaborate on points you will get marks that way as well.

Answer

Twin studies involve comparing MZ and DZ twins on the basis that MZ twins share 100% of their genes and DZ share 50% of their genes, so any difference in concordance between the two types of twin is said to be down to genes. The problem is that both sets of twins share their environment too; however, identical twins (MZ) might share their environment more because, looking identical, they are treated more similarly than DZ twins. ✔ Twin studies are used to say that a characteristic is down to nature. However, this is hard to prove even with twin studies because no characteristic appears in MZ twins 100% of the time so there must be environmental causes as well, which are hard to control for. ✔ Twin studies are reasonably valid because they involve simply looking for characteristics rather than manipulating variables, so they tend to be about real-life characteristics. ✔ However, if the studies are about something like IQ then there is testing. It is hard to know exactly what is being tested as perhaps there are different types of IQ, so studies to that extent might not be valid. ✔

🖉 Other features of twin studies could be that MZ twins are unique and it is hard to generalise to other twins or to the rest of the population. Also sometimes 'identical' twins are not MZ twins as records can be wrong. However, the points above are enough for the marks to be given and each point is clearly and thoroughly made.

■ ■ ■

Content

(1) The biological approach gives more than one explanation for gender differences. Describe one biological explanation for gender differences. (4 marks, AO1)

🖉 This is a straightforward question asking you to give one way that the approach explains gender. You need to make four clear points although if you elaborate on a point you will get more marks for it.

Answer

Genes dictate gender differences from conception. ✔ (*identification mark*) The mother contributes an X chromosome and the father contributes either an X or a Y chromosome. ✔ An XY combination will produce a male baby and an XX combination will produce a female baby. ✔ The single chromosome strand from the egg fits with the single chromosome strand from the sperm and a new strand of DNA is formed. The DNA triggers proteins that set off certain processes. ✔ For example, at about 6 weeks the fetus is the same whether male or female, but then hormone production starts to make a difference. Androgens and MIS mean that male genitalia develop, for example. ✔ The genes trigger certain hormones.

🖉 There are 5 ticks here as the answer is thorough. The first mark is given for a short first sentence but this is an identification mark for the biological explanation. An identification mark is not always given for such a question so it is a good idea to give enough detail for 4 marks without the identification mark, as is done here.

(2) Explain what is meant by the nature–nurture debate. (2 marks, AO1)

[?] There are just 2 marks here so the answer can be fairly brief. You could get 1 mark for a brief definition of the debate and 2 marks for a more thorough one.

Answer

Something is said to come from nature when it is biologically given and a person or animal is born with that characteristic. ✔ Something is said to come from nurture if it comes from environmental influences rather than in the 'nature' of the person or animal. ✔ The debate is whether a certain characteristic comes from nature, nurture or some combination. ✔

[?] Both 'nature' and 'nurture' are explained in sufficient detail for the 1 mark each. If there were more marks available you could give an example for each to add to the explanation. Then the final mark is for explaining the debate.

■ ■ ■

Studies in detail

(1) Outline the procedure of two studies in the biological approach. (6 marks, AO1)

[?] For two studies outline the procedure for 3 marks each. You will have studied Money (1975) and one other; in this book Raine et al. (1997) is the other study so it is used here, but you can use a different study. Note that the Money study is a case study, so for the procedure just outline what was done. This is the case description.

Answer 1

Money (1975) found that a genetic male could be brought up successfully as a female and Raine et al. (1997) found that murderers' brains were different in some ways compared to a control group.

Answer 2

Money (1975) carried out a case study where he gathered evidence from the parents and child concerned. The child was born a male and had an identical twin brother but then a circumcision operation had gone wrong and the penis had been ablated. ✔ The parents were unsure what to do and had contacted Money to ask for advice. Money had been working with people who had had their sex reassigned, including children, and he suggested bringing the boy up as a girl. ✔ The study documents the child's progress as a girl for 9 years, until the 'girl' was about 11 years old. ✔ Raine at al. (1997) had access to 41 people who had been charged with murder or manslaughter and who were pleading not guilty by reason of insanity. ✔ They put together a matched control group. Then they used PET scanning to obtain evidence about the brains of the 82 people and measured glucose activity as well as looking at other brain areas using the scan pictures. ✔✔

✏ Answer 1 gets 0 marks because it is about results and not procedure.

✏ Answer 2 gets all the marks. It is not hard to allocate the 3 marks for the Money study as there is probably more than enough material. However, there is only just enough material for the 3 marks for the Raine et al. study. The short comment about matching a control group could have done with more detail, such as about the six schizophrenic participants, but the last sentence has quite a bit of information so the comment about the control group is put with that to give a double mark.

(2) Evaluate Money's (1975) study.   (4 marks, AO2)

✏ This question does not ask for description so just give evaluation points. A detailed point will get 2 marks or you can give four separate evaluation points. Consider such issues as ethics, validity, reliability and generalisability.

Answer

Money (1975) concluded that the girl had been successfully brought up as a girl and saw herself as a girl. However, the individual concerned later made himself known and explained that he had always felt wrong and had reverted to being male which was how he felt more comfortable. So the findings of the Money study were not valid. ✔ A case study is often not reliable either because it cannot be repeated and this particular case study could not be repeated. It is unlikely that a situation like it would happen again for the findings to be replicated. ✔ This also means that as the situation was unique the findings cannot be generalised to the rest of the population. ✔ For a long time the study was used to show that nurture is powerful. Now the study is used to show the complete opposite, that nature is powerful. The study can be criticised with regard to the ethics as the people involved, including the parents and the two sons, seem to have been badly affected by events, to the extent that the two sons have committed suicide. ✔

✏ In this answer enough is said for the 4 marks, but if there were more marks available it would get more for its good use of terms such as reliability, validity and generalisability and for the amount of relevant material.

■ ■ ■

Key issue

(1)   Tim's parents were worried about his behaviour even though he was only 4 years old. He played on his own all the time and he tended to choose one particular game with his toy cars that he played for hours, rarely varying

what he was doing. He gave little eye contact with his parents or his older sister and showed very few emotions. His parents thought this was not normal. Tim was very inflexible as well, and stuck to very strict rules with regard to what he would eat and how he did things. He enjoyed setting things in order and the game he played with his cars involved ordering them for size and colour. His older sister, however, was completely different, being very sociable and having lots of friends. His parents took Tim to a specialist, who said he thought Tim was autistic and explained that one theory about autism was that it meant Tim had an extreme male brain.

Using concepts and ideas from the biological approach, explain why Tim was diagnosed as autistic and why the specialist made the comment about the male brain. In your answer bring in evidence from the stimulus material. (6 marks, AO2)

This is a long extract to show you the sort of question that can be asked about a key issue (in this case, about the issue used in this guide). You have to bring in what you have learned in the approach and relate that to parts of the extract. There are 6 marks available so you need to make a good number of points. The reason a lot of detail is given in the extract about Tim's abilities and preferences, and his sister's, is that a candidate would not be expected to have studied autism but would be able to pick things out of the extract about genes and brain structures that are linked to gender.

Answer

Tim shows that he likes systems and order (such as in his car game) and his sister has more friends and is more sociable. This links with what studies have shown about male and female brains. Males use the right side of the brain more, which is for visuospatial tasks and would be for systems and maths too. ✔ Females use both sides more than males, and tend to use the left brain, which is for language. Females are supposed to be better at reading body language and emotions, again showing brain differences from males, who are not good at these tasks. ✔ Tim did not show emotions nor did he relate well to members of his family, which shows a male brain trait. ✔ However, males can show and read emotions, just not as much as females, whereas in Tim the difference is extreme. ✔ (This sort of evidence has led Simon Baron-Cohen to suggest that autism is evidence of an extreme male brain, which is what the specialist in the extract is referring to. ✔ Tim is withdrawn as well, a strong trait of those with autism. Autism appears in more males than females, with about four males to every one female. ✔ There is an autistic spectrum too, which means some people show some autistic tendencies though not as much, such as those with Asperger's syndrome. For Asperger's syndrome there are about ten males to every female.) The biological approach suggests that male and female brain differences can come from different levels of testosterone, with males having high levels of testosterone. ✔ (There is also an explanation of autism that it is genetic, but there is nothing in the extract that suggests this as there is no mention of other family members having those tendencies. ✔) It is hard to say whether a characteristic such as autism is nature or nurture because both affect every child and cannot be separated for us to study them. ✔

📝 There are nine ticks given here as there is a lot of detail — more than enough for 6 marks. The final tick is for an evaluation point about methodology and finding out about autism. The last but one tick is for mentioning that autism might be genetic. These two ticks are not precisely focused on autism as extreme male brain but act as evaluation or additional points. The other ticks are all for talking about the theory, including one mark for linking to Baron Cohen, which shows a good level of learning. The bracketed material could only be given by a candidate who had studied autism, but there are 6 marks in the unbracketed material to show that enough can be given from the approach itself. The 'specialist' material is here to help you write a different key issue answer.

■ ■ ■

Practical

Within the biological approach you will have carried out a test of difference. Answer the following questions with your practical in mind.

(1) (a) Give the aim of your study. (1 mark, AO3)

📝 For your practical expect to give the aim as this makes it clear what your study was about.

Answer

The aim of my study was to see if females are better at language tasks then males. ✔

📝 This is clear and fine for the 1 mark available.

(b) Give the null hypothesis. (2 marks, AO3)

📝 One mark would be given for a basic null hypothesis and 2 marks for a full one. A hypothesis should refer to both the IV and the DV, for example.

Answer

There is no significant difference between males and females in the number of anagrams they can solve in 3 minutes, and any difference there is, is due to chance. ✔✔

📝 This is fine for the 2 marks. The null is about there being no difference or relationship, so this hypothesis is accurate. The IV (gender) and the DV (how many anagrams are solved in the time) are both given clearly.

(c) **Give three reasons for choosing a Mann Whitney U test for your study.**

(3 marks, AO3)

There is a standard way of answering this sort of question, so it is useful to learn this off by heart. Consider whether the study is about a difference or a correlation, what the design is and what the level of measurement is.

Answer

The design is independent groups, ✔the data are interval ✔ (how many anagrams solved) and this is a test of difference ✔ not a correlation, so a suitable test is a Mann Whitney U test.

This answer is fine for all 3 marks as three elements are covered.

(d) **Evaluate your study in terms of its validity.**

(2 marks, AO3)

There are just 2 marks here for saying how 'real life' your study was. You could consider whether the setting and/or the task were realistic.

Answer

For my DV I measured how many anagrams the person could solve in a set time, and this is not a very realistic task. The task was to test for language ability whereas solving anagrams is only one specific part of using words, so validity can be queried. The task was done in the school common room, which is in a way the participants' (students) natural setting, so perhaps there was ecological validity. ✔✔

This is more than enough for the 2 marks. The comments about the task are enough for 2 marks and the comments about the ecological validity are perhaps just enough for 2 marks as well, though it would be better to add more about what ecological validity means to make sure.

(e) **What does it mean to say that a test has to be a one-tailed test?** (1 mark, AO3)

The answer has to be a definition of what one-tailed means.

Answer

One-tailed means that the hypothesis does not give the direction the results will go in.

This is not right: the answer defines two-tailed, not one-tailed. Be careful to answer the question set.

(f) **Explain one control that you put into place and explain why.** (3 marks, AO3)

Giving one control you used would gain 1 mark. The other 2 marks are for either explaining your control in more detail or expanding clearly on why it was important.

Answer

I made sure that all the participants, both male and female, used the same list of anagrams. ✔ Not just the same list of muddled words, but printed in exactly the same way and presented as the timer was pressed. ✔ There had to be nothing about the list that was different for the two groups, to make sure that any difference in the number solved had to be due to the IV, which was gender, rather than to differences in the lists. ✔ Everything else had to be the same.

📝 This answer gets 2 marks for the actual control, which is clearly explained, and then the further mark for the reason for this control, which is clear even though it would be the reason for any control — that everything but the IV has to be the same. Your answer should relate to your study and not be general.

(g) **What sampling method did you use and what was one advantage or disadvantage of using this method?** (3 marks, AO3)

📝 There is 1 mark for the sampling method and 2 more marks for either an advantage or a disadvantage: 1 mark for a brief explanation and 2 marks for a thorough one.

Answer

I used opportunity sampling. ✔ A disadvantage of this is that not everyone in the chosen population has the chance of being chosen. This is biased sampling because I only used students from my college. ✔ Also I only used students who were in the common room on the day of my study. Again only those that agreed were participants and I probably only approached those I got on with. ✔ So there is quite a bit of bias in the sample.

📝 For full marks, there needs to be quite a bit of information, which this answer provides. It relates clearly to the actual study, which is important. Avoid giving a 'general' answer to this question — make sure that the advantage or disadvantage connects to your own study (e.g. the mention of 'college' and 'students' in this case). There might not be a mark for just the name of the sampling method because it is likely that everyone will say 'opportunity' sampling. But the mark is given here because the rest of the answer makes clear that it was an opportunity sample.

Section **3**

The learning approach

Definitions

(1) For each of the types of learning — classical, operant and social learning — give a real-life example of how learning would take place. (6 marks, AO1)

> This is rather unusual as a question. When defining any term it is suggested that you use an example to show understanding. Here you are asked to focus just on examples, with 2 marks available for each: 1 mark for a simple one and 2 marks if it is explained more fully.

Answer

An example of classical conditioning is being afraid of lifts. Being trapped can give an automatic example of fear. Being trapped in a lift can transfer that basic fear to lifts. ✔✔ An example of operant conditioning is a dog barking for a biscuit. When the dog first barks, the reward of a biscuit is given and soon the dog learns to bark for the reward, which is positive conditioning. ✔✔ An example of social learning is a small girl brushing her hair like her mother brushes her hair. The behaviour would come from the girl observing her mother and then performing the observed behaviour. ✔✔

> In all three cases an example is given and explained in relation to the learning theory, so full marks.

(2) Define what is meant by extinction and spontaneous recovery with regard to classical conditioning. (4 marks, AO1)

> There are 2 marks for each definition, with 1 mark for a brief answer and 2 marks for a more thorough answer.

Answer

Extinction occurs when a previously learned association no longer produces the response to the stimulus. This happens after the pairing no longer occurs for a while — the stimulus then does not produce the response. ✔✔ However, sometimes for no apparent reason the stimulus, after extinction, starts producing the response again, which is called spontaneous recovery. The response appears spontaneously, which means not planned, and so is recovered. ✔✔

> There is enough information in both cases for all the marks. It can be hard to see where the ticks would go, because you are not giving two things for the 2 marks in each case, but a rich and detailed definition gets them.

■ ■ ■

Methodology

(1) Describe and evaluate observation as a research method in psychology.

(12 marks, AO3)

🖉 This is an essay question. It is more likely to be asked in a different way, but it is good practice for you to answer such straightforward essay titles. If you do not evaluate, your marks will be limited to about half marks. To reach the top marks you need to communicate well, using relevant terms correctly and giving a well-balanced answer.

Answer

Observations can be overt, which means those being observed are aware of the study, or they can be covert, which means they are not aware that they are being studied. Participant observation means that the observer is part of the situation. Non-participant observation means that the observer is set apart from the situation. So there are these different combinations when naturalistic observations are carried out. Observations can gather qualitative data when open questions are asked such as making notes about someone's opinions. And they can gather quantitative data, such as tallying certain behaviours like children playing with a certain toy. Often both types of data are collected. A strength of observations is when more than one observer watches the same behaviour, using the same categories, because if their observations match there is inter-observer reliability. Also if it is a participant observation there can be good validity, as the observer can access all the data and it is 'real life' — which is the good point about naturalistic observations. One problem can be that generalisability is difficult because a naturalistic observation tends to be about one group of participants, and a different group can yield different data because there are fewer controls than there are in an experiment.

🖉 More could be said here, but the length is limited to show what can be included in quite a short answer (for 12 marks). A strength is that when a point is made to describe or evaluate, it is a complete point. For example, the answer does not just say that observations are valid, it explains why. It is important that when you make a point you show knowledge with understanding — that you show, for example, that you know what a term means. This answer is in the top level, gaining perhaps 10 of the 12 marks. A little more evaluation is needed, in talking about reliability for example, though inter-observer reliability is clear. More could have been said to link validity to naturalistic observations.

(2) **An observation of helping behaviour in a shopping mall showed that more males than females held doors open for other shoppers. Tallying was carried out, recording not only the gender of those helping (holding the door open for someone else) but also the gender of those being helped (those going through the door). It was necessary only to record helping behaviour when**

one person held the door and one person came through, so if more than one person came through that incident was not recorded. No other information was recorded, such as whether the person being helped was carrying heavy shopping or not. A test was done on the results, which were found not to be significant at $p \leq 0.05$.

Table of results for the study showing number of those helping and those helped with regard to gender

Gender of person being helped	Gender of helper		
	Male	Female	Total
Male	12	4	16
Female	18	8	26
Total	30	12	42

(a) **What test would be needed for this study? Give three reasons why this would be the test chosen.** (4 marks, AO3)

> You would get 1 mark for naming the test and 1 mark for each reason. Remember to focus on whether the test is for a difference or a relationship, what the design is and what the level of measurement is.

Answer

The test is the Chi-squared. ✔ This is the test for looking for a difference ✔ when the data are nominal ✔ and it is an independent groups design. ✔

> This shows how you can pick up marks quickly if you learn the methodology carefully. This answer gets all 4 marks.

(b) **Give one example of where a control would have been useful.** (2 marks, AO3)

> There are problems built in to the study, so pick one of these and show how it should have been controlled. Show real understanding and you will get the 2 marks.

Answer

It would have been useful to know whether the shopper was weighed down with bags or not, as this could have made people more likely to hold the door open regardless of gender and was a possibly extraneous variable that needed to be noted or controlled. ✔✔

> This is a good point — it is important to record all data in an observation, otherwise conclusions might be wrongly drawn; by missing out detail there was a possible other reason for any findings. The answer has enough detail for the 2 marks.

(c) Explain one ethical issue with this study. (2 marks, AO3)

> 🗩 You need to think carefully about this answer, because naturalistic observations are special with regard to ethics.

Answer

One problem with observations is that there can be no informed consent, so the study is always going to be unethical. BPS guidelines ask for informed consent for every study.

> 🗩 This answer gains no marks because observations are permitted if the behaviour occurs in a public place where someone expects to be observed, which is the case here. It would often not be possible to carry out observations otherwise. If someone is in the public eye and all other ethical issues are observed, then observing them without recording personal information is seen as ethical.

(d) The test was found not to be significant, at $p \leq 0.05$. Explain what this means.

(2 marks, AO3)

> 🗩 This question is about levels of significance. Explain what the phrase $p \leq 0.05$ means and what it means to say the study is not significant at that level.

Answer

The phrase $p \leq 0.05$ means that the probability that the results are due to chance is equal to or less than 5%. ✔ Saying that the results are not significant at that level means there is a greater than 5% probability of the results being due to chance so the null hypothesis would not be rejected. ✔

> 🗩 This gains the marks as the answer shows clear understanding of the 5% level of significance and what it means to say that that level is not achieved.

(e) Did more males help than females overall? (1 mark, AO3)

> 🗩 This is a simple question to test understanding of figures and tables. Expect some questions like this. There is no catch to it. Refer to the figures in the table.

Answer

More males than females helped overall, with 30 males helping compared with 12 females. ✔

> 🗩 This is clear and the right answer. The results show that more males helped than females and more females were helped than males.

■ ■ ■

3

section

Content

(1) For either classical or operant conditioning, evaluate one therapy. (4 marks, AO2)

🖉 This is about evaluating a therapy not describing it, so make sure you only make evaluation points. Either give four evaluation points or elaborate on fewer. It is probably wise when revising to prepare four evaluation points.

Answer

Systematic desensitisation is more ethical than other treatments for phobias because it is a gradual treatment rather than exposing someone to something they most fear, which would cause a lot of distress. ✔ It has also been shown to be successful by studies such as Capafons et al., who used it to cure people of their phobia of flying and it helped in overcoming this fear. ✔ However, the treatment is only successful for those who are able to relax successfully and maintain that relaxation, which might not apply to everyone. ✔ Also it is not a treatment that rests only on classical conditioning as claimed, because it involves cognitive elements such as positive thinking while relaxing. ✔

🖉 This answer gets all 4 marks and the points are thoroughly made. Perhaps more of Capafons et al.'s evidence would make the point even more clearly, as would more about the cognitive elements.

(2) Compare one or more learning theory explanation for gender development with one explanation from one of the other approaches. (4 marks, AO2)

🖉 This question asks you to evaluate learning theory explanations together with one different explanation. There are no marks for describing the explanations but some element of description would be needed, as it is hard to evaluate without describing when the evaluation skill asked for is 'compare'.

Answer

Social learning theory suggests that gender behaviour is learned by observing role models and imitating their behaviour. This is about learning from the environment, whereas biological explanations suggest that gender behaviour comes from 'nature'. ✔ Operant conditioning suggests that gender behaviour comes from being rewarded for behaviour, which again means that environmental rewards govern gender behaviour. ✔ (*elaboration point*) This shows how learning explanations are about nurture and the experiences people undergo, whereas the biological approach suggests that there is a genetic blueprint that governs behaviour including gender behaviour. ✔ Genes trigger hormones and the brain develops differently as well, so there are these three aspects to gender development according to the biological approach, and all these are about nature not nurture and so are different from the two learning theories briefly outlined. ✔

🖉 This answer gets the 4 marks and shows that you need a lot of detail to get the marks, although in practice you are likely to get marks more quickly than this answer suggests. Prepare a lot of detail for 'compare' questions — these are the questions that discriminate between candidates and show how well you understand the material. The answer could alternatively have compared with psychodynamic explanations. It could also have mentioned that the biological approach does involve the environment to an extent — environment in the womb and influences that affect genetic triggers.

■ ■ ■

Studies in detail

(1) Outline the aim(s) of two of the following studies: Bandura, Ross and Ross (1961), Watson and Rayner (1920), Skinner (1948) and Pickens and Thomson (1968).

(4 marks, AO1)

🖉 The studies used in the answer here are Bandura, Ross and Ross (1961) and Skinner (1948). If you chose one of the others, use that when answering this question. The 2 marks for each study are: 1 mark for a brief aim and another mark either for more detail or for another aim for the same study. With Bandura et al. (1961) make the aim very clear because a general aim could apply to other social learning theory studies as well and you would then not get the marks. For example, saying that the aim was to see if children copy aggression would not be enough.

Answer

The aim of Bandura, Ross and Ross (1961) was to see if children imitate adult models depending on whether they show aggressive or non-aggressive behaviour, and depending on whether the model is male or female and the child is a boy or a girl. ✔✔ The aim of Skinner (1948) was to see if pigeons would show behaviour that they happened to be displaying when a reward was given, even though the behaviour was not deliberately reinforced. ✔✔

🖉 Both aims get 2 marks as they are specific. They are also detailed enough to show which study they refer to even if the name of the study were not given, which is something to aim for in your answer.

(2) Compare the findings of Bandura, Ross and Ross (1961) with one of the following studies: Watson and Rayner (1920), Skinner (1948) and Pickens and Thomson (1968).

(4 marks, AO2)

🖉 The question asks you to look at the results or conclusions or both of the two studies. This answer uses Skinner (1948), but if you have revised one of the other

two you could use that. In order to compare the studies you could look at the methodology, including perhaps ethics, and how this affects the findings. Or you could examine the findings themselves to see if they differ or are at all comparable. From the point of view of methodology this is an AO3 question, but looking at the findings makes it AO2.

Answer

Both Bandura, Ross and Ross (1961) and Skinner (1948) are laboratory studies, which makes them similar as they both have at least one IV and a DV that is measured. This makes the findings reliable in both cases. ✔ However, the Bandura study uses children as participants and the Skinner study uses pigeons, so one is about animal learning and one is about children's learning, which makes them different. It might be more possible to generalise the findings from children to other children and humans, as Bandura et al. wish to do, than to generalise findings from pigeons to human learning, which is what Skinner did in his operant conditioning theory. ✔✔ Skinner's theory is reasonably ethical as he used the minimum number of pigeons (8) as ethical guidelines for animals suggest. Also, although he made sure the pigeons were hungry he only partly starved them (they were still at 75% of their body weight) and not for a long time. Bandura et al.'s study is ethical in that the children were in a reasonably natural setting and confidentiality was ensured. However, the children were exposed to an aggressive role model, which might be seen as unethical. So perhaps Skinner's findings are more ethically achieved than Bandura et al.'s. ✔✔

A thorough answer which gets the full 4 marks. There are 5 ticks to show how thorough this answer is, as there is enough for more than 4 marks. Note that in each case the mark is given when the findings are mentioned. Comparing the methods by saying they are both laboratory experiments does not relate precisely to the findings, so it is good that the answer then comments about reliability, which does refer to the findings. The marks are given after the findings are linked in, but where the comment is given in a lot of detail 2 marks are awarded. The answer uses terminology such as generalisability, reliability, confidentiality, role models, IV and DV. Bringing in key terms makes double marks more likely.

■ ■ ■

Key issue

(1) Identify an issue that can be explained using concepts from the learning approach. Then explain it using two concepts from the approach. (7 marks, AO1/AO2)

This question gets AO1 marks although it probably entails AO2. It depends on whether you have prepared the answer, in which case it is knowledge and AO1, or whether you have to apply the concepts yourself, in which case it is AO2.

Answer

One issue is whether role models have an influence on whether someone develops anorexia or not. ✔ One concept from the learning approach is identification. When someone identifies with a role model they are likely to imitate their behaviour. ✔ Studies by Bandura have shown that girls copy female models and boys copy male models, so if female role models are slim then girls are likely to want to be slim. ✔ If someone observes behaviour but does not identify with the role model they are not so likely to perform the behaviour. ✔ Girls who want to be slim are likely to stop eating and can develop eating disorders such as anorexia. Another concept from the learning approach is reinforcement. If a role model is reinforced for being slim, such as praised, paid more or featured a lot in the media, then they might be imitated more. ✔ Studies by Bandura have shown that behaviour that is rewarded is likely to be imitated more, such as in vicarious learning. ✔ There is also negative reinforcement for being fat, through criticism and teasing. So not wanting to be fat to avoid criticism, and wanting to be slim to get praise, might be two types of reinforcement that help to explain anorexia. ✔

🖉 All 7 marks are given: 1 mark for identifying the issue, 3 marks for discussing identification and 3 marks for discussing reinforcement. The answer is good because the two concepts are different enough to be easy to mark. If the answer had looked at identification and then imitation, it would have been harder to unravel, although marks would of course have been given. Choose two concepts that are quite different if you can.

■ ■ ■

Practical

You will have carried out an observation within the learning approach. Answer the following questions using your study.

(1) (a) How did you gather the quantitative data when doing the observation?

(2 marks, AO3)

🖉 This question asks about how you measured and gathered the numbers for the study. Make sure you talk about quantitative data and are precise about the study.

Answer

I made tally marks according to the gender of any child playing in the book corner and the gender of any child playing on the climbing frame. There was one mark for each act of playing in those ways, and the mark went in the relevant gender box, boy or girl. ✔✔

🖉 This is detailed and clear. Every incidence of playing in the book corner and playing on the climbing frame is detailed. The problem is knowing how often the tally marks

are made if the same child continues to play in the same way. From this account it is assumed that there is one mark per child, no matter how long the play continues. Assuming this is the case, then this answer is detailed. The examiner will assume that the answer is true. The answer only tests that you know how to do what you did, not that you actually did it.

(b) What was the independent variable (IV)?   (1 mark, AO3)

> There is 1 mark here for the IV. Remember to give the IV in full, not just one part of it.

Answer

The IV was gender — whether a child was a boy or a girl. ✔

> In this case the two sides of the IV are covered by the one word 'gender', though this is not usually the case with an IV. This answer sensibly expands the point to make sure of the mark.

(c) To what extent was your study credible?   (4 marks, AO3)

> This question requires an in-depth look at credibility and the credibility of your study. Make sure your explanations are clear. Credibility can be split into two parts. There is subjective credibility, which is about how believable something is in terms of people's usual experiences. And there is objective credibility, which is about how firm the evidence for something is, including how scientifically the evidence was gathered. Make sure you relate this clearly to your own study at least once rather than giving an answer focusing on what credibility is or on studies in general.

Answer

My study is credible because the research method was scientific, in that quantitative data were gathered. ✔ Quantitative data can be measured in such a way that the study can be repeated so the findings can be tested for reliability. ✔ This is particularly the case if there is more than one observer and they agree, though in my study there was only me so this might mean the study is not so credible. ✔ Also quantitative data can be analysed using statistical testing, which is a scientific way of finding out to what extent the results are due to chance. ✔ My study is also credible in that it is widely believed that girls play with 'girls' toys' and boys with 'boys' toys' and that girls prefer language tasks such as playing in the book corner, with boys preferring climbing. For example, in advertising there is often a picture of a boy on a box with an activity toy inside. ✔

> This answer gets five ticks so there are more points than are needed for the 4 marks. The answer is rather general about reliability, statistical testing and objective data, but that aspect is directly linked to this person's study by the comment that there was only one observer. The final comment about the results matching what is expected ('face validity') gets a mark as it is about credibility in

the subjective sense. The 'matching expectations' element of the last part of the answer is implied clearly enough to get the mark.

(d) What sampling method did you use? (1 mark, AO3)

🖉 Guessing what your sampling method was, you might like to put 'opportunity' here as, first, it is probably true, and, second, there is no way in this set of questions for the examiner to see if the answer is true, so you would get the mark anyway. This question on its own, therefore, is unlikely to be asked.

Answer

Opportunity. ✔

(e) Explain one problem with your study. (3 marks, AO3)

🖉 You could use a problem that you solved or you could use a problem that you did not deal with. 'With your study' is sufficiently vague to allow for both these interpretations.

Answer

One problem with my study was working out which child was a boy and which was a girl when doing my observation. ✔ I observed children aged between 3 and 4 and they were often dressed in trousers. It was not clear from hair cuts either which were boys and which were girls. ✔ I had to ask a member of staff where I was not sure. I tried to note down something about the child such as colour of jumper and then asked staff later. However, this might have meant my tallying was not always accurate, which would have affected the study. ✔

🖉 Not only is the problem clear but the explanation of how the problem might have affected the findings is also clear, as well as what was done about the problem. This is a thorough answer and gets the full 3 marks.